Other books by Witold Rybczynski

Paper Heroes

Taming the Tiger

Home

The Most Beautiful House in the World

Waiting for the Weekend

Looking Around

A Place for Art

City Life

The Perfect House

A Clearing in the Distance

One Good Turn

Last Harvest

My Two Polish Grandfathers

MAKESHIFT METROPOLIS

IDEAS ABOUT CITIES

Witold Rybczynski

SCRIBNER

New York   London   Toronto   Sydney

SCRIBNER
A Division of Simon & Schuster, Inc.
1230 Avenue of the Americas
New York, NY 10020

First Scribner hardcover edition November 2010

SCRIBNER and design are registered trademarks of The Gale Group, Inc.
used under license by Simon & Schuster, Inc., the publisher of this work.

For information about special discounts for bulk purchases,
please contact Simon & Schuster Special Sales at 1-866-506-1949
or business@simonandschuster.com.

The Simon & Schuster Speakers Bureau can bring authors to your live event.
For more information or to book an event contact the Simon & Schuster Speakers
Bureau at 1-866-248-3049 or visit our website at www.simonspeakers.com.

DESIGNED BY ERICH HOBBING

Manufactured in the United States of America

1   3   5   7   9   10   8   6   4   2

Library of Congress Control Number: 2010030285

ISBN 978-1-4165-6126-2

To
Martin Meyerson (1922–2007),
city planner, teacher, valued colleague,
and
Martin Pawley (1938–2008),
fellow garbage architect, writer, friend.

The city is a fact in nature, like a cave, a run of mackerel, or an ant heap. But it is also a conscious work of art, and it holds within its communal framework many simpler and more personal forms of art.

—Lewis Mumford

But what we have to express in expressing our cities is not to be scorned. Their intricate order—a manifestation of the freedom of countless numbers of people to make and carry out countless plans—is in many ways a great wonder.

—Jane Jacobs

Contents

Preface

Like those of many architecture students of my generation, my ideas about cities were formed by reading Lewis Mumford and Jane Jacobs. While I pored over their books, in class and out, I was too green to see that in many important ways they were intellectual adversaries. Mumford, wistfully looking back at the preindustrial city, actively promoted a small-scale urban future planned according to the teachings of his mentor, Patrick Geddes. Jacobs, suspicious of planning in general and contemporary planning in particular, saw the city as having its own rules, rules that planners had largely ignored or, in the case of modern visionaries—including Geddes—willfully usurped. I met Mumford once briefly, at a group lunch when he visited McGill University. He had witnessed the creation of modern architecture and planning, which gave him an almost mythic aura. A courtly gentleman, he was formal and somewhat distant, a figure from another age. Jacobs, iconoclastic, feisty, and outspoken, was much more appealing to an impressionable tyro.

A half century has passed since Jacobs wrote *The Death and Life of Great American Cities*, and the years have tempered my unseasoned judgments. Her offhanded dismissal of the City Beautiful and the Garden City, for example, now seems a little too easy; both movements left an indelible—and positive—imprint on American cities. Her perceptive analysis of street life is circumscribed by what we have since learned about defensible space and community policing. And the urban world has changed in the last fifty years: the gradual disappearance of manufacturing has altered the face of many "great" American cities; poverty and racial division in inner-city neighborhoods persist; and suburban and exurban sprawl have become important engines of metropolitan growth. At the same time, a growing awareness of environmental issues has revived interest in Mumford's call for regional planning.

The debate between Jacobs and Mumford needs to be understood in a historical context, and chapter 2 explores the three chief ideas that influenced American city planning during the first half of the twentieth century: the City Beautiful, the Garden City, and the Radiant City. Chapter 3 details the mighty attack on modern planning mounted by Jacobs, and its momentous influence on the design professions. However, at the same time as she focused attention on the state of downtown, American urbanism was following the decentralizing course that Frank Lloyd Wright had anticipated thirty years earlier with Broadacre City, a suburban vision so far beneath Jacobs's contempt that her book simply ignored it. Chapter 4 describes how Wright, an idiosyncratic genius, turned out to be a prophetic seer. Chapter 5 weaves these strands together and demonstrates how the three ideas—and Jacobs's critique—have played out in the evolving American city, reemerging as waterfront parks and new varieties of garden city suburbs. As for Wright's expansive vision of an ever-spreading urban frontier, reality has long since surpassed his expectation.

PREFACE

The American city as an unplanned, almost anarchic arena for individual enterprise—a makeshift metropolis—has, in many ways, fulfilled Jacobs's vision. Yet, it has done so in unexpected ways. The most successful urban neighborhoods have attracted not the blue-collar families that she celebrated, but the rich and the young. The urban vitality that she espoused—and correctly saw as a barometer of healthy city life—has found new expressions, in planned commercial and residential developments, whose scale rivals that of the urban renewal of which she was so critical. These developments are the work of real estate entrepreneurs, who were absent from the Jacobite city described in *Death and Life*, but loom large today, having long ago replaced planners as our chief urban strategists.

This book summarizes what I have learned about city planning and urban development. Sixteen years ago I started teaching an introductory class in design and development to MBAs and real estate majors. I got to know my colleagues—predominantly economists—in the real estate department of the Wharton School. Without exception, I found them committed to urban research, studying housing, public finance, immigration, and urban poverty. Their overarching interest in the city is not so different from that of the architects and city planners in the School of Design, where I also teach; all share a common concern for improving cities and the lives of the people who live and work in them. But economists assume that to propose changes, you must first understand how things work. Consequently, their research is concerned less with what the city *should* be than with what it actually is—how it functions. This means gathering and analyzing vast amounts of data, trying to understand why people behave the way they do, live where they live, choose what they choose.

Although planning projects typically start with a functional analysis and an investigation of site conditions, traffic patterns, and so on, the main goal of the urban designer is to discover a novel physical solution to the problem at hand. Architects and planners are concerned with what they believe cities should be: safer, denser, greener, more diverse, more lively. The working assumption is that the designer—who is, after all, the expert— has the interests of the users in mind and knows best how to achieve these worthy goals. In contrast, my economist colleagues are working on the problem from the other end, trying to discover what people themselves actually want.

Is a city the result of design intentions, or of market forces, or a bit of both? These are the questions I explore in this book. Chapters 6 and 7 chronicle a sort of alternative urban history, one that is concerned with the demands of users, consumers, and entrepreneurs, rather than with planners' prescriptions. The antagonism between the current fad for building signature architecture, the so-called Bilbao Effect, and urban design is recounted in chapter 8. Chapter 9 is an account of what we have learned about building and rebuilding cities, and how the lessons of the past fifty years appear to be coalescing into strategies that combine pragmatism and piecemeal development with public and private actions. The final two chapters contrast the kind of cities that Americans want, and the kind of cities that the present environmental crisis suggests that we need, which turn out to be not at all the same. Resolving this contradiction is the prime challenge for the next generation of city builders.

MAKESHIFT METROPOLIS

1

Remaking the City

I am standing on the roof of a building overlooking the Brook-lyn waterfront. It's March, and a bitterly cold wind blows off the river, but the sun is shining brightly, and the view of towering Manhattan across the sparkling waters of the East River is splen-did. "Each one of these piers covers five acres," my companion, landscape architect Michael Van Valkenburgh, tells me, "that's the size of Bryant Park." Van Valkenburgh's enthusiasm is con-tagious as he describes the highlights of a public park that will eventually stretch more than a mile along the waterfront, from Atlantic Avenue in the south to beyond the Brooklyn and Man-hattan bridges in the north. For now, the area resembles an abandoned parking lot, with cracked paving and piles of debris behind a sagging chain-link fence. Traffic along the Brooklyn-Queens Expressway creates a steady drone. Although demoli-tion of the old pier sheds is complete, it's hard to imagine this place as a park, but Van Valkenburgh assures me that it will be largely complete in four years. The first truckloads of earth will arrive next week.

The four-story building we're standing on houses Van Valkenburgh's site office, where he and his partner Matt Urbanski explain the project to me with the aid of a fifty-foot-long model that takes up most of the loftlike space. What the model depicts doesn't look much like a traditional park. A narrow strip of land along the shore is filled with model trees made out of a green, spongy material, but about a third of the park is located on six cargo-shipping piers, rectangular platforms that stick out into the river like fingers. One of the piers will be used for baseball and soccer fields, three will be covered by lawns and wildflower meadows, one will house courts for basketball, handball, and tennis, and the sixth will be a wildlife sanctuary. Van Valkenburgh and Urbanski describe a rich variety of amenities, not just game-playing areas and jogging trails but also nature paths for hiking, tidal pools for wading (the river here has a four-foot tide), a large calm-water basin for kayaking, beaches for sunbathing, picnic areas, dog runs, a small-boat marina, as well as an outdoor market and a water-taxi landing. All this on only eighty-five acres.

Public parks are a distinctive feature of North American cities. Not the manicured green squares and tame pieces of garden art of Europe, but large expanses of make-believe countryside, with lakes, rivers, meadows, and forests. Most of these parks date from the second half of the nineteenth century, and the individual most responsible for influencing public attitudes at the time and showing how parks should be designed and built was Frederick Law Olmsted. Olmsted's parks, especially Prospect Park in Brooklyn and Central Park in Manhattan, were immensely popular, and the idea that a large park was an urban necessity quickly spread across the continent—to Buffalo, Montreal,

A park grows in Brooklyn.

Chicago, Philadelphia, Boston, San Francisco, Louisville, and scores of smaller cities.

Van Valkenburgh, like all American park builders, is following in Olmsted's footsteps. But while Central Park was promoted by business leaders, large landowners, and politicians, Brooklyn Bridge Park is the result of a neighborhood initiative. In 1988, residents of Brooklyn Heights, which overlooks the site, founded the Brooklyn Bridge Park Conservancy to oppose a proposal by the Port Authority to develop the waterfront as commercial real estate; the conservancy lobbied for a public park instead. (Despite the presence of Prospect Park, Brooklyn has the least amount of parkland of any major metropolitan area in the country.) A compromise was struck. The city would build a park, but the project would have to finance itself, both parties agreeing that as much as 20 percent of the site could be devoted to revenue-generating nonpark uses such as housing.* The income would go directly to the Brooklyn Bridge Park Development Corporation, which would oversee park upkeep—estimated to be about $15 million a year (maintaining piers is expensive). In 1998, during the planning, Van Valkenburgh's firm was brought in as a consultant, and following a design competition he was named planner and lead designer of the park.[1]

As we walk around the site, Van Valkenburgh describes the three chief design challenges, which all derive, in one way or another, from the adjacent Brooklyn-Queens Expressway. Fifty years ago, when Robert Moses was building the expressway, to mollify Brooklyn Heights residents and reduce noise his engineers covered the two-level elevated highway with a pedestrian deck. The resulting Brooklyn Heights Promenade became a much beloved feature of the neighborhood and has since been designated a historic landmark. This has a major impact on the proposed park, since the designation legally requires that the spectacular view of Manhattan from the promenade be protected by a so-called view plane, into which no new building may protrude. The view plane extends over the entire central portion of the future park, which means that new high-rise construction can only occur at the southern and northern tips of the site. Van Valkenburgh and his team have used this limi-

---

*The final master plan devotes only 10 percent of the site to private development.

tation to solve the park's second big problem: the expressway effectively blocks direct access from Brooklyn Heights along the entire central portion of the park. By concentrating development at the two ends—a hotel and apartment buildings on the north, and apartment buildings (adjacent to a disused furniture factory that has already been converted into condominiums) on the south—the planners not only respect the view plane, but also create what they call "urban junctions," entrances to the park that they hope will become lively links to the adjacent neighborhoods. At the same time, the limited access means the park has to become a *destination*, that is, a place with unique attractions of its own. "It's got to be worth a long subway ride or a trip in the car," says Van Valkenburgh. Hence the kayaking basin, the extensive waterfront picnicking areas, and the large playing fields, all rare amenities in Brooklyn.

The third challenge is noise. The Brooklyn-Queens Expressway was specifically designed with a curved back wall to reflect the noise of traffic away from Brooklyn Heights and toward the river—precisely into the area that will be the future park. To deaden the noise, the landscape architects have planned an earthen berm along the entire length of the expressway. The lower portion of the berm is gently sloped to allow human use; then it's steep at the top to make it as tall as possible. The steepest section, built with stabilized earth, will not be accessible to the public. Fencing off a part of the park sounds odd, but Van Valkenburgh reminds me that large portions of traditional parks such as Central Park are not accessible to the public and are there simply to "create a setting." The main setting of Brooklyn Bridge Park is the harbor, eight hundred acres of water that will make the park seem much larger than it is.

Most of the structures in the park—fences, benches, lighting—will have a rough-and-ready appearance, which Van Valkenburgh describes as contributing to the industrial "authenticity" of the site. Piers capable of supporting heavy loads will be sodded, while others will remain paved; those in poor condition have been demolished. When restoration of the sole surviving nineteenth-century railroad pier, where freight was transferred between ships and railroad cars, proved too costly, it was decided to let soil accumulation and plant establishment continue naturally, turning the collapsed pier into a habitat for nesting birds. In a curious bit of ecological engineering, to prevent rats from decimating the fledglings, the front of the pier will be demolished to make an island. The pier closest to the Brooklyn Bridge was originally built on landfill, so it will be heavily planted with trees, creating a coastal forest. On another pier, the steel framework of a cargo shed has been retained to support a new shading roof over playing courts. Where decrepit retaining walls must be torn down, the water's edge will be turned into beaches, tidal pools, and boat-launching areas; solid quay walls will support promenades. In the site office, Urbanski shows me a slab of heavy, dense wood—Southern yellow pine—a large quantity of which was recovered during the demolition of one of the industrial sheds. The seasoned, weather-resistant timber will be recycled to construct benches, screen walls, and other park structures. A mock-up of a section of fencing, made of galvanized metal pipe, stretched steel cable, and a metal screen, reminds me of a cargo net.

Olmsted and his partner Calvert Vaux drew people into Central Park by introducing boating and ice-skating, as well as musical concerts; Van Valkenburgh and his team continue this

An unexpected urban pastime: kayaking in the East River.

tradition of active and passive recreation, except that instead of Victorian gazebos and bandstands, there will be basketball courts and giant screens for outdoor movies. The combination of private real estate development and public uses at Brooklyn Bridge Park has struck some critics as anomalous, but it, too, has a precedent in Olmsted, who argued that the fiscal advantage of building public parks was precisely that they raised adjacent property values and increased city revenues. In other areas, modern landscape architects have moved beyond their predecessors. The designs of Central Park, Prospect Park, and others were based, in part, on the re-creation of idealized natural landscapes, some British, some American, hence the Sheep Meadow and the "wild" Ramble of Central Park, and the picturesque man-made lake and the Adirondack-like Ravine of Prospect Park. The landscapes that Van Valkenburgh and his team will create in Brooklyn are a product of their waterfront location and will include a coastal scrubland, freshwater wetlands, and marsh and shallow-water habitats. "We attempted to work closely with site conditions to use these natural zones to jump-start a functioning ecology that will eventually take on a life of its own, with relatively minimal intervention," Van Valkenburgh explains. Whereas park designers of Olmsted's generation saw their creations as an antidote to the surrounding industrial city, Van Valkenburgh sees Brooklyn Bridge Park as an integral part of its urban surroundings.

The planning of Brooklyn Bridge Park involves on-the-spot improvisation: reacting to immediate neighborhood concerns, dealing with difficult site conditions, respecting stringent financial constraints, making do with what is at hand. Van Valkenburgh has described the landscape architect's goal as "a combination of understanding the things that are givens and then setting it up in a way so that the occurrence of the undeterminable is a welcome consequence."[2] Yet his pragmatic approach, no less than Olmsted's, is guided by ideals—concerning ecology, community, planning, and urbanism. Big ideas and practical schemes: a new chapter in remaking the makeshift American metropolis is unfolding.

Cities don't grow in a vacuum. Urbanism is conditioned by what came before, not only physically but also intellectually. To better understand the possibilities and constraints for planning, it's helpful first to examine three key concepts that have shaped the way we think about urbanism and that have helped make our cities what they are today.

2

Three Big Ideas

Town planning in America began auspiciously in the eigh-
teenth century with colonial settlements such as New Haven,
Philadelphia, Annapolis, Williamsburg, and the sublime
Savannah, all laid out according to precise rules, with care-
fully ordered streets, avenues, squares, and town greens. Who
planned these cities? The author of New Haven's unusual nine-
square plan, like a tic-tac-toe diagram, with space for a market
in the center square, is unknown; it may have been Theophilus
Eaton, one of the leaders of the group of Massachusetts settlers
who founded the town (originally called Quinnipiac), or John
Brockett, the group's surveyor. While the entire plan of New
Haven measured only half a mile square, the ambitious plan
of Philadelphia covered one mile by two. The streets were laid
out in a regular grid divided into four quadrants by two inter-
secting major streets, with a public square in each quadrant
and one in the center. The planner was the Pennsylvania colony's surveyor general, Captain Thomas Holme, who is generally described as an engineer and may have learned that skill

in the military, although William Penn, the colony's governor, almost certainly contributed to the plan. Farther south, the governor of Maryland, Francis Nicholson, devised the exceptional plan of his new capital, Annapolis. The urbane arrangement included four open spaces: two circular squares (which predate John Wood's Circus at Bath by more than thirty years)—Public Circle and Church Circle—a residential square, and a marketplace. Streets radiated diagonally from the circular squares in a miniature version of baroque Rome.

Nicholson had an opportunity to plan a second city when he was appointed governor of Virginia. The result was Williamsburg, which one historian has called "the most successful essay in community planning of colonial America."[1] While the plan of Annapolis leaned heavily on European antecedents, Williamsburg is more original, a wide main street forming the chief axis of the plan. The College of William and Mary stands at one end, and the Capitol at the other. Midway between them is a market square, originally also the site of the courthouse and a powder magazine. The other major building of the town is the governor's palace, which Nicholson sited at the head of a tree-lined green that extended at right angles to the main street. The plan has two striking features: the houses are on generous lots surrounded by gardens, and the lots along the main street are interrupted by shallow ravines. The result, architect and planner Jaquelin T. Robertson writes, is a plan that provides "a clear American order of things, elegantly canonizing the format of our public buildings, streets, houses, trees, yards and natural terrain."[2]

The planner of Savannah was James Oglethorpe, founder and governor of the Georgia colony. Oglethorpe, who had been a successful general in the English army, was also a social reformer, settling the new colony with "working poor" and banning slavery. His remarkable town plan was based on a standardized "ward" consisting of forty house lots surrounding a central square fronted by public buildings. As the town grew, new wards were added in an orderly fashion. This sounds mechanical, but the ingenuity of the plan was that major and minor streets were an integral part of the expansion, creating continuous, treed avenues that connected the wards. Of all the colonial plans, this was not only the most sophisticated, but also the most long-lived, since Oglethorpe's pattern guided the city's growth from its founding in 1733 until the Civil War.

Most colonial towns lacked the finesse of Savannah and Williamsburg, however. Alexandria, Virginia, founded in 1749, was typical. Eighty-four identical half-acre lots were arranged four lots per block, with the streets forming a simple grid that was inelegantly truncated by the irregular shoreline of the Potomac River. This no-frills subdivision was laid out by John West Jr., a surveyor, and his assistant, seventeen-year-old George Washington. Forty years later, President Washington had to decide on a plan for the nearby federal capital. His secretary of state, Thomas Jefferson, a recognized expert on all matters architectural, suggested an Alexandria-like grid and even submitted a rough sketch. Washington forwarded the drawing to one of his advisers, who responded with a withering critique: "Such regular plans indeed, however answerable they may appear upon paper or seducing as they may be on the first aspect to the eyes of some people must even when applied upon the ground the best calculated to admit of it become at last tiresome and insipid and it never could be in its origin but a mean continuance of some cool imagination wanting a sense of the real grand and truly beautiful only to be met with where nature contributes with art and diversifies the objects."[3] The author of this rant was a young Frenchman, Pierre-Charles L'Enfant. He had come to America to fight in the Revolutionary War and served on Washington's staff, rising to the rank of major. On the strength of his artistic abilities (he remodeled New York's Federal Hall, where Washington had taken the oath of office), the president commissioned him to prepare a topographic drawing of the site of the future federal city. Impressed with L'Enfant's evident enthusiasm and convinced by his argument that the new capital should be "grand and beautiful," Washington subsequently entrusted him with the planning of the capital city.

L'Enfant is sometimes described as an architect or a military engineer. He was neither; immediately before leaving France he had been an art student. But he could draw, he had an innate understanding of city planning, and he was immensely ambitious. His plan for the federal capital had three chief characteristics: it took advantage of the topography by locating the Capitol on one hill, the President's House on another, with a Grand Avenue (today the Mall) leading to the Potomac; diagonal avenues, clearly influenced by French garden design, linked the prominent civic buildings and created many *rond-points* at the intersections for commemorative statues; and a matter-of-fact grid of secondary streets was superimposed on the diagonal avenues. The plan was, as one historian has put it, an "American balance of precedent and innovation."[4]

During the early years of the nineteenth century, L'Enfant's plan influenced a number of new cities. Buffalo, New York, then called New Amsterdam, was laid out with long diagonals radiating from a public square near the shore of Lake Erie by Joseph Ellicott, the brother of Andrew Ellicott, who succeeded L'Enfant as the planner of the federal capital. The plans of cities such as Indianapolis, Baton Rouge, Cleveland, Madison, Wisconsin, and Sandusky, Ohio, all show L'Enfant's influence, as do many smaller settlements whose layouts historian John Reps wittily characterized as "backwoods baroque."[5]

The most novel post-Washington city plan was undoubtedly that of Detroit, laid out by Judge Augustus Woodward in 1807. Woodward knew L'Enfant and devised an unusual variation of the radiating-avenue plan: an octagonal pattern of streets and avenues resembling a honeycomb. Woodward's scheme is barely discernible today; however, for within a decade of Detroit's founding, the city fathers had abandoned the octagonal plan in favor of a rectilinear grid. Throughout the nineteenth century, as settlement moved westward, and as established cities grew larger, despite the early experiments, the grid became the preferred American planning model. The grid-planner required no artistic training and simply imposed his plan without regard for topography, as San Francisco and Pittsburgh demonstrate. All that a budding city-builder needed was to decide on street widths and the distance between intersections; the rest followed automatically. Blocks were filled in by private builders—an office building here, a tenement there, manufacturing lofts, public libraries, department stores, places of worship, playhouses, warehouses—whatever was needed at the time. The sentiments fueling this pragmatism were a combination of democratic egalitarianism—the proverbial level playing field—an emphasis on entrepreneurship rather than aesthetics, and a kind of laziness.

Yet, ideas—and even ideals—were never entirely absent, as the parks movement of the nineteenth century demonstrates. During the first half of the twentieth century, cities came under the sway of three big ideas: Charles Mulford Robinson's national crusade for urban beautification; Ebenezer Howard's notion of the Garden City; and Le Corbusier's image of towers in a park. These men were unlikely urban visionaries: an upstate New York newspaperman who wrote the first American book on city planning; a British parliamentary stenographer and failed Nebraska homesteader, whose ideas gave birth to an international movement; and a Swiss-born artist-architect who fancied himself a city planner and, against all odds, changed the face of cities in a country that he barely knew. To understand the way we live—and plan—today, it is necessary to appreciate the extent to which these three visionaries influenced American ideas of city life.

CHARLES MULFORD ROBINSON AND CIVIC ART

A great awakening of civic awareness took place in America during the first three decades of the twentieth century. The most obvious surviving artifacts from this creative period are the magnificent public buildings, constructed of marble and granite and decorated with monumental art, that adorn most major cities. Daniel H. Burnham's imposing Union Station in Washington, D.C., is a model of the type, combining solidity and urbanity with an unparalleled self-confidence. It's not just that the train station is substantial and clearly built to last, with white granite walls, gold-leaf decorations, and bronze

Charles Mulford Robinson,
godfather of the City Beautiful
movement, c. 1915.

fixtures. Whenever I walk through the tall, vaulted waiting room, beneath the somber statues of brooding warriors, and out into the arched loggia across from the Capitol dome, I have the distinct impression not only of arrival, but also of a shared sense of civic engagement.

The public celebration of urban beauty, as demonstrated by Union Station, was in large part the idea of a man who was neither an architect nor a planner. Charles Mulford Robinson was born in 1869, not in a city but in a small town, Ramapo, New York. He grew up in a well-to-do family in Rochester, where he went to university and worked as a journalist and freelance writer on a wide range of topics: a history of the city, a privately published biography of his great-grandfather Judge Augustus Porter, as well as the libretto of an operetta based on Robin Hood. In

1899, he published a three-part series in the *Atlantic Monthly*, simply titled "Improvement in City Life." The improvement that Robinson described was chiefly artistic, but he approached his subject broadly: "When one speaks of the aesthetic side of American cities, one thinks at once of their public buildings; of their parks, statues, and boulevards. But in any right conception of urban loveliness these would be only the special objects of a general and harmonious beauty."[6] He might have been writing about Philadelphia, where he later worked as associate editor of the *Public Ledger,* the city's largest daily. Although Philadelphia had a monumental new city hall and a large park along the Schuylkill River, as well as a recently built fountain dominated by an enormous equestrian statue of George Washington, its tight Colonial grid was being overwhelmed by commercial buildings and factories, and its business center was disfigured by the elevated tracks of the Pennsylvania Railroad.

In the *Atlantic* series, Robinson took the broadest possible view of what he called civic art and discussed practical ameliorations such as limiting the height of buildings, removing advertising, cleaning streets, planting trees, improving lighting, and installing public art. He cited numerous examples of civic improvements in various American cities: a Chicago ordinance restricting billboards adjacent to boulevards and parks; a New York initiative to keep city streets clean; a successful public effort in Boston to preserve the historic façade of the state capitol. In other words, he described how cities could be made more attractive. He emphasized that while city governments sometimes took the lead in these improvements, a variety of private organizations, such as municipal art societies, park associations, and civic clubs, also had roles to play, in a way that anticipated today's park conservancies and downtown business-improvement districts. Robinson observed that although these various efforts were diversified, widely scattered, and lacking in harmony, there were also attempts to treat conditions in a manner that was more "scientific."[7]

The following year, William Dean Howells, the editor of *Harper's Magazine,* invited Robinson to write about city beautification in Europe. Robinson visited Paris, Brussels, and London and produced another three-part series.[8] Like many Americans who traveled to Europe, he was impressed by the beauty of its cities and realized that despite America's wealth and growing world influence, its cities did not really measure up. In 1901, he assembled his urban essays in a small book, *The Improvement of Towns and Cities,* and followed it two years later with a detailed study of the subject, the masterful *Modern Civic Art.* What makes the latter so compelling is a combination of close observation and common sense; sixty years later, even the demanding urban historian and critic Lewis Mumford considered Robinson's book "an excellent book in its time and still worth consulting."[9]

Robinson was interested in aesthetics, but his view of the city was not that of an aesthete. "Cities are not made to be looked at, but to be lived in," he wrote.[10] "The wish for a beautiful street will remain always visionary until the want is felt of a good street and a clean one."[11] He emphasized the importance of establishing the architectural character of a city and called for more attention to be paid to city halls and courthouses— "people's houses," he called them. He wrote that outlying residential neighborhoods should have "broad streets and narrow streets, straight and curving ways, and regularly built up districts sprinkled through with open spaces, where there may be playgrounds for children or gardens for the delight of all."[12] Nor did he ignore those parts of American cities that needed the most improvement.

> In the wealthier portions of the city there may be imposing plazas, broad avenues, and noble sites crowned with worthy structures; public architecture may reach a high level of good taste and luxury, and domestic architecture may be fittingly expressive of the spirit of the time, revealing, under professional guidance, at once variety and harmony; but until the spirit of aesthetic renaissance descends into the slums and gives play to artistic impulse there, the conquest of beauty in the city will be still incomplete.[13]

Robinson's articles and books are the first in twentieth-century America—certainly the first addressed to a wide audience—to argue the need for city planning. "We shall not attain to cities really beautiful, then, until we learn artistically to plan them," he wrote.[14] This was an implicit criticism of the nineteenth-century laissez-faire attitude that had been adopted by American city-builders, who had forgotten—or ignored—the achievements of an earlier generation. Even the great Olmsted, who pioneered the idea of vast city parks, assumed that they would be surrounded by distinctly unlovely cities. That was not good enough for Robinson.

Robinson wrote with a wide readership in mind, and his ambition came to fruition as his ideas were taken up and propagated by an array of national organizations, including the American Civic Association, the American League for Civic

Improvement, and the American Park and Outdoor Art Association, in all three of which he was an active board member. Civic beautification was also promoted by various professional associations, including the newly founded American Society of Landscape Architects, and by scores of local groups, chambers of commerce, businessmen's clubs, and municipal societies. Some of these groups acted out of a sense of civic duty, others responded to Robinson's economic argument—familiar to modern ears—that beautification would attract businesses to their city.

The emerging national interest in civic improvement that Robinson described and actively promoted is generally referred to as the City Beautiful movement.[15] Although Robinson himself coined the term in his *Atlantic* series, he used it sparingly and preferred *civic art*, which carried with it a sense of public-spiritedness.* Nevertheless, it was *city beautiful* that stuck in the popular imagination, not least because it captured a particular aspect of civic art—beauty—that had recently come to the fore, thanks to two well-publicized national events.

The first was the World's Columbian Exposition, which took place in Chicago in the summer of 1893. Although the fair, planned by Frederick Law Olmsted, included a gaudy carnival midway and a naturalistic lake and island, its showpiece was the Court of Honor, a large water basin surrounded by a group of monumental buildings designed by half a dozen of the country's leading architects. Popularly known as the White City, because of the uniform white color of the architecture, this part of the

---

*Although the term *civic art* has gone out of fashion, it was once widely used. One of the important reference books on city planning (published in 1922), *The American Vitruvius*, was subtitled "An Architects' Handbook of Civic Art."

The World's Columbian Exposition of 1893
showed Americans their urban future.

fair resembled an urban civic center. Robert A. M. Stern has called the Court of Honor "the first effectively planned complex of public buildings built in America since the Jeffersonian era" (referring to Jefferson's University of Virginia campus), and for the 27 million visitors to the fair it was an eye-opener.[16] The unmistakable message of the White City was that American cities could be planned—beautifully and grandly. Robinson wrote an illustrated guide to the fair, in which he recognized its national significance. America was growing wealthier, he wrote, people's horizons were being expanded by travel, and what he called the "provisions of the essentials of life" had been vastly increased for the majority of the population.[17] All these changes would be felt in the city.

Although the Chicago fair included an eclectic collection of pavilions, from the Colonial Revival Pennsylvania Building, which resembled Independence Hall, to Louis Sullivan's poly-

The era of civic landmarks: Union Station
in Washington, D.C.

chrome Transportation Building, the architecture of the Court
of Honor itself was uniform. The buildings that surrounded
the huge reflecting pool were in a style loosely based on the
Italian Renaissance. Several of the architects—Richard Morris Hunt, Charles McKim, and Robert Peabody—as well as the
sculptors Augustus Saint-Gaudens and Frederick MacMonnies,
had studied at the École des Beaux-Arts in Paris, the world's
leading center of Classical teaching. These men, and the fair's
chief architect, Daniel Burnham, believed that the Classical
tradition, adapted to American circumstances, was an appropriate model for cities in the burgeoning republic. Burnham
and his colleagues, like many American architects and artists,
saw the arrival of the United States on the world stage as anal-
ogous to the rebirth of European culture during the Renaissance. In any case, as historian Vincent Scully points out, it is
hardly surprising that American architects adopted the grand

manner of Beaux Arts city planning, since it represented the "only model for complete, or almost complete, urbanistic form" available to them.[18] A later generation would characterize the Beaux Arts architecture of the fair as retrograde, but that misses the point; the Chicago exposition publicly and convincingly demonstrated the merits of planning and urban beautification, both distinctly novel concepts at the time.

The second national event that paved the way for the City Beautiful movement occurred seven years later. In 1900, the U.S. Senate established a commission to prepare a comprehensive plan for the monumental core of the city of Washington. The members of what is often called the McMillan Commission, since it reported to Senator James McMillan, had all worked together on the World's Columbian Exposition: Daniel Burnham, the young Frederick Law Olmsted Jr. (son of the famous, now retired, landscape architect), Charles McKim, and Augustus Saint-Gaudens. In 1902, they unveiled a new plan for the nation's capital, described in a series of dramatic watercolor views and two giant scale models of central Washington, illustrating conditions "before" and "after." The McMillan Plan reconfigured and expanded the Mall, consolidated the Federal Triangle, and established sites for Union Station and the Lincoln and Jefferson memorials.[19] Although Burnham, Olmsted, and McKim claimed L'Enfant's plan as a precedent, their design was solidly in the grand Beaux Arts tradition, with geometrical axes, symmetrical building arrangements, monumental public sculpture, and stylistic consistency. The new center of Washington, D.C.—now truly a White City—is the most prominent achievement of the architectural epoch that came to be known as the American Renaissance.

Although the popular successes of the Chicago exposition and the McMillan Plan linked the City Beautiful idea to Classical architecture in the public's mind, Robinson did not discuss architectural style in his writing. He was catholic in his taste (although he disliked skyscrapers), asking only that architects exercise self-restraint. "The need is that [the architect] should realize that his problem is not that of a building only, but of a city," he advised.[20] Always good advice. However, while Robinson sensibly recommended variety in urban architecture, what the leading architects of the day generally delivered was uniformity—Classical buildings with Classical ornament and uniformly grand Classical colonnades. Thus, in practice, the city beautiful became the city monumental, which somewhat compromised Robinson's balanced vision of a heterogeneous urbanism—and provided fodder for later critics.

Thanks to his writing, Robinson became a national figure and was engaged as a planning consultant by a number of cities, including Sacramento, Santa Barbara, Fort Wayne, Denver, Des Moines, Omaha, and Honolulu. He was part of the team that designed a "Model City" for the popular 1904 Saint Louis World's Fair; served on planning commissions in Rochester, New York, and Columbus, Ohio; and was appointed professor of civic design at the University of Illinois at Urbana-Champaign, one of only two universities in the United States to offer courses in city planning (Harvard was the other). He continued to write and in 1916 published the well-received *City Planning*, recommended by the *New York Times* in its list of "leading spring books."[21]

Robinson's whirlwind activism was cut short in 1917, when he died of pneumonia, only forty-eight years old. Earlier that year he had written a new preface for the fourth edition of *Modern Civic Art*. "Many of the hopes (or possibly visions) expressed in the First Edition have become actualities," he wrote, "some observed tendencies toward better things are now established movements; and many specific conditions, which then were criticized, now have been corrected."[22] His optimism was entirely justified, for the decades immediately before and after his death were a time of great accomplishments in urban beautification. In 1910, Congress created the Commission of Fine Arts to oversee the implementation of the McMillan Plan, and in the next decade some of the plan's key elements, such as the rebuilt Mall and the Lincoln Memorial, were realized. A series of national fairs, in Saint Louis, San Francisco, and San Diego, continued the Chicago exposition's example of complete urban ensembles, exposing the American public to city-planning ideas. Burnham's ambitious master plan for San Francisco was short-circuited by the great 1906 earthquake and fire, but John Galen Howard's design for a new civic center complex followed the City Beautiful model. Burnham and Edward H. Bennett's *Plan of Chicago* was the most detailed master plan for any American city to date, although it was in some ways theoretical. Even larger in scale was a study of recreational areas in Los Angeles, prepared by Olmsted Jr. and planner Harland Bartholomew. Covering fifteen hundred square miles, the far-thinking forty-year regional plan called for acquiring several hundred million dollars' worth of land for parks, playgrounds, and beaches.[23] The proposal is distinctive for recognizing the particular character of Southern Californian urbanism: people lived mainly in individual houses, and their chief means of transportation—this was just 1930—was the private automobile.

While the Los Angeles recreational plan was stillborn, thanks to a lack of political will and the Great Depression, other planning projects were realized. John C. Olmsted, Frederick Law Olmsted Jr.'s older half brother, laid out a citywide park system for Seattle. Monumental groups of government buildings appeared in state capitals in Colorado, Nebraska, Wisconsin, and Pennsylvania. In an early—though more successful—version of what would later be called "urban renewal," downtown beautification schemes were undertaken in Detroit, Cleveland, Pittsburgh, and Philadelphia. A host of new urban college campuses—Johns Hopkins in Baltimore, Rice in Houston, Southern Methodist in Dallas, California Institute of Technology in Los Angeles, the University of Colorado in Boulder, and the Army War College in Washington, D.C.—were planned along City Beautiful lines. Monumental train stations were built in New York, Philadelphia, Kansas City, Dallas, Los Angeles, and Washington, D.C. Even as late an urban project as Rockefeller Center in New York, despite its Art Deco style, owes a debt to the City Beautiful. All told, the movement left an extraordinarily rich legacy of urban improvement.

Robinson's ideal of civic art dominated American city planning and architecture for three productive decades, until the twin disruptions of the Great Depression and the Second World War.* Rare is the American city that does not have at least one example of Robinson's civic ideal: a grand museum or train sta-

---

*The period 1900–1930 was blessed with an overabundance of talented designers interested in the city: not only giants such as Burnham and McKim, but also great landscape architects and planners such as the Olmsted brothers, Warren Manning, John Nolen, and Jacques Gréber, and architects of the caliber of Ralph Adams Cram, Thomas Hastings, Paul Philippe Cret, and Henry Bacon.

The era of civic landmarks: The New York Public Library.

tion, a park or a parkway, a monumental urban square. Indeed, subtract the City Beautiful achievements of 1900–1930, and most American cities would be vastly diminished. In New York City, for example, there would be no Columbia University or New York University campuses, no U.S. Post Office on Eighth Avenue (still impressive, though bereft of its grander twin, Pennsylvania Station), no Municipal Building in downtown Manhattan, no Grand Central Station, no New York Central Building straddling Park Avenue, and no New York Public Library. The library, a paragon of how a civic building should take its place in the city, is a reminder that while planning theories come and go, their built expressions survive for a long time. Not many people remember Charles Mulford Robinson today, but anybody who sits on the broad library steps under the marble lions

Patience and Fortitude, the casual passerby on Fifth Avenue, and every lunchtime visitor to Bryant Park is experiencing Robinson's vision of civic art.

EBENEZER HOWARD, THE GARDEN CITY GEYSER

Although Charles Robinson referred to "the science of modern city-making," city planning is not a science but a practical art, and it developed in fits and starts. No one was a more unlikely contributor to this haphazard process than Ebenezer Howard. Born in 1850 in London to a family of modest means and apprenticed as a clerk, he decided to immigrate to the United States and become a farmer. He and two friends chose Nebraska, but the hard conditions quickly brought an end to their naive experiment, and Howard found himself stranded in Chicago, forced to work as a court reporter to earn his passage home. It was the early 1870s, and the city was just recovering from the Great Fire, so Howard had the rare opportunity to see entire urban neighborhoods being built from scratch. Not that Chicago was rebuilding itself in a particularly unusual way. As often happens after urban disasters, the old street plan was maintained and new buildings simply took the place of the destroyed ones. The skyscrapers that would make Chicago a world leader in tall buildings were still a decade off, but the frenzy of reconstruction that gripped the city must have made a strong impression on the young Englishman.

The most important lessons that Howard drew from his four-year American experience were that cities not only could be built anew, but also could be built differently than in the past.

In 1868, Frederick Law Olmsted and Calvert Vaux had planned a new residential community nine miles west of the Loop. Riverside, as Olmsted named it, was one of the first—and certainly the largest—planned suburban communities in the United States, probably in the world: twenty-five hundred individual building lots on sixteen hundred acres of Midwestern prairie. "The idea," according to Olmsted, "being to suggest and imply leisure, contemplativeness and happy tranquility."[24] By the 1870s, Riverside was in its infancy, but it already exhibited the environmental qualities that set it apart from conventional American cities and towns: individual houses on spacious half-acre lots, winding country roads instead of gridded streets, thousands of newly planted trees, and many public green spaces. The development gave the impression of a vast park rather than an urban neighborhood. There is no direct evidence that Howard visited Riverside, but it seems likely that he was aware of the project, and it would have pointed him in the direction of a new type of urban living, dispersed and bucolic.

When Howard returned to London, he got a job as a parliamentary stenographer, married, started a family, and began what promised to be an unremarkable life. Small indications of the adventurous spirit that had taken him to the American frontier were his hobbies: he dabbled in new inventions, especially typewriters; was interested in spiritualism; was fluent in Esperanto; and was an active member of a local debating society, where he met the socialist Sydney Webb and the young George Bernard Shaw.

The Remington Company was a leading manufacturer of typewriters, which Howard occasionally visited in the United States. During one trip he came across *Looking Backward*, a novel written in 1888 by Edward Bellamy, a Massachusetts lawyer. The plot concerns a Bostonian who falls asleep and wakes up in the year 2000 to a dramatically transformed society. Bellamy came from a family of socialists, and in his futurist Utopia all human needs were benignly filled by state-owned industries. Bellamy's vision of Boston in the year 2000 was in stark contrast to the industrial cities of his day: "Miles of broad streets, shaded by trees and lined with fine buildings . . . stretched in every direction. Every quarter contained large open squares filled with trees, among which statues glistened and fountains flashed in the late afternoon sun."[25] *Looking Backward* was enormously popular, selling a million copies, and more than 150 "Bellamy clubs" sprang up nationwide, and the political impact of the book has been compared to that of *Uncle Tom's Cabin*. Bellamy spent the last ten years of his life promoting his version of socialism and helping to found the Nationalist party, which advocated state capitalism.

Although Howard did not share Bellamy's somewhat authoritarian views on how society should be organized politically, he was attracted to the author's reformist urban vision, particularly the notion of public ownership of land. Indeed, Howard was so taken by the book that he arranged for a British edition and personally distributed a hundred copies to friends. But while Bellamy advocated wholesale political change on a national scale, Howard, whom Lewis Mumford once described as a "practical idealist," started thinking about how a community organized along the lines that Bellamy described might actually be implemented—not in some vague Utopian future, but at that very moment, in Britain.

During the late 1880s Howard collected his ideas in a small

book that was published as *To-morrow!: A Peaceful Path to Real Reform*. Howard's book is a detailed blueprint for a new city that combines the advantages of town and country. His detailed economic calculations rested on three assumptions: first, that all the land in the city would be owned by a public corporation; second, that the corporation would buy cheap agricultural land, improve it, and reinvest future profits in the new city; and third, that the size of the city would be limited to thirty-two thousand inhabitants. He called the community Garden City, perhaps inspired by Chicago's motto, *Urbs in Horto*—City in a Garden. In 1902, when the book was reprinted, he changed the title to *Garden Cities of To-morrow*.

Although Howard was not an architect, he included a schematic plan of his proposed city. Garden City strongly resembles an exercise in civic art, and American influences are plentiful: there is a Central Park, and a linear green avenue resembling Chicago's Midway; broad boulevards recall the parkways that Olmsted laid out in Brooklyn; and the avenues are numbered, just as in New York City. The most original architectural feature was the Crystal Palace, a continuous glass-roofed, arcaded mall that contained the commercial district of the town. Because of its small size, the city was walkable—the only mass transit was a municipal railway connecting it to neighboring garden cities.

One of the streets in the plan was named Edison Street, and Garden City is very much the work of a solitary inventor: a curious mixture of quirky innovation, pedantic analysis, and detailed calculation. Howard, an unprepossessing man, was an unexpectedly effective public speaker and a tireless proselytizer—Shaw called him "Ebenezer the Garden City Geyser"—and to promote his ideas he organized the Garden City

Sir Ebenezer Howard,
inventor of the Garden City.

Association, whose membership soon spread across Britain.[26] In 1902, he helped found a company that acquired a tract of land and built the first garden city, named Letchworth. Letchworth was planned by Raymond Unwin and his partner Barry Parker. Unwin, the son of a Nonconformist Oxford tutor, was a follower of William Morris and a committed socialist. He and Parker were both early members of the Garden City Association and had already planned an industrial village when they won an architectural competition to design Letchworth. Like the City Beautiful architects, Unwin, who became the leading architect and planner of the Garden City movement, believed that beauty was an indispensable part of town planning. But, although he studied large cities such as Paris and Berlin, his model was not baroque Rome but rather the domestic architecture and haphazard plans of medieval towns and villages.[27]

The function of Letchworth and the garden cities that fol-

PROPOSED SHOPS · HAMPSTEAD GARDEN SUBURB ·

The model Garden City suburb: Hampstead Garden Suburb,
near London, c. 1909.

lowed—indeed, their chief attraction—was to serve as alternatives to the crowded industrial city. However, none of the garden cities that were built achieved the economic autonomy that Howard envisioned. Instead they invariably depended for employment on a nearby metropolis. Hampstead Garden Suburb, planned by Unwin and Parker in 1905 and connected to London by an underground railway, has been described as a "glorious composition of buildings, streets and landscape as complex and subtle as any in the history of architecture" and is the prototype Garden City suburb.[28] The entire development, which is next to Hampstead Heath, ultimately covered more than seven hundred acres, with innovative housing quadrangles designed by Unwin and Parker, as well as groups of houses by such leading British architects as M. H. Baillie Scott and Edwin Lutyens. Hampstead was suburban in location but townlike in appearance, with a mixture of houses and apartment buildings, as well as a town center with a central square. The community roughly followed Unwin's rule of "twelve houses to the acre," which was much less dense than industrial cities at that time.

Howard died in 1928. Knighted by King George V, celebrated as Britain's leading exponent of city planning, he lived long enough to see Garden City associations spring up across Europe, where the terms *Gartenstädte*, *cité-jardin*, and *ciudad-jardín* entered the lexicon. Garden City developments were built in Germany, France, and Holland, and even as far away as Palestine. And, not least, in America. By a curious historical coincidence, the Garden City idea was introduced to the United States by the son of the very man whose suburban planned community—Riverside—had influenced the young Howard in Chicago. By the early 1900s, Frederick Law Olmsted Jr. had achieved a prominence in the profession of landscape architecture that rivaled his father's. He established the country's first landscape architecture program, at Harvard, was a member of the Commission of Fine Arts, a founder and president of the American Society of Landscape Architects, and the first president of the American City Planning Institute. His firm, Olmsted Brothers, which he ran with his half brother John, was the largest and best known in the country, responsible for not only landscape architecture but also town planning. The latter interest took Olmsted, in 1908, to Germany, Holland, France, and Britain, on a three-month tour of Garden City developments. While he was in Germany, he received a letter from a prospective client. "We are proposing to go into housing on a fairly large scale, in the suburban district of New York," wrote philanthropist Robert Weeks de Forest, on behalf of the Russell Sage Foundation. "Our plan is not merely to give houses but to lay out these tracts in some way different from the abhorrent rectangular city block, and to make our *garden city* [emphasis added] somewhat attractive by the treatment and planting of our streets, the possibility of little gardens, and possibly some public spaces."[29] Olmsted responded immediately, "Nothing could interest me more than such a problem as you have on hand."[30] Thus began America's first Garden City, Forest Hills Gardens.

The 142-acre site of Forest Hills Gardens was in the borough of Queens, linked to Manhattan by the newly electrified Long Island Rail Road. The projected population of five thousand was to be housed largely in detached single-family homes, but also in apartment buildings, row houses, and twins. Although Olmsted was influenced by what he had recently seen in Germany and Britain—and by the picturesque principles he had learned from his father—what he produced was entirely original. Opposite the railroad station, he laid out a town square to serve as a commercial center. Behind the square he placed a village green, and leading away from it two so-called greenways, which snaked their way through the community to terminate in a large existing park. The plan was thus a subtly orchestrated transition from urban to pastoral. Although the residential streets connected to the surrounding New York grid, they were anything but gridlike; Olmsted created a variety of crescents, internal circles, lanes, and closes, laid out with all the design artistry that a talented and experienced planner could bring to bear.[31]

Forest Hills Gardens is only a fifteen-minute ride from Penn Station. Getting off the train and descending an outdoor staircase into Station Square, I find myself in a cobblestoned place

A garden suburb in the city: Station Square,
Forest Hills Gardens, in New York.

surrounded by buildings with deep arcades, half-timbered walls infilled with patterned brick, and steeply pitched red-tile roofs topped by clock towers and turrets. The overall effect recalls a medieval Bavarian town, perhaps Rothenburg, which was much admired by Garden City planners and architects. Behind the arcades are shops, restaurants, and professional offices; above, apartments. Most of the buildings have three or four stories, with one section rising to nine stories. The towerlike building was originally the Forest Hills Inn, which functioned as the social heart of the community, a sort of vertical country club.

The inn and the other buildings around Station Square are the work of Grosvenor Atterbury, an established New York architect who was a friend of de Forest's and had built a summer-house for him at Cold Spring Harbor.[32] At Forest Hills, Atterbury designed not only the buildings around Station Square but also the train station, a church, a new home for the West Side Tennis Club (where the U.S. Open was held until 1978), and a number of house groups and individual houses. The ornamental iron streetlamps and street signs that dot the community are also his work and attest to the Arts and Crafts sensibility that he brought to the project. The German medieval style of Station Square was unusual for Atterbury, but like most of his contemporaries, the Beaux Arts–trained architect was able to work in a variety of styles, depending on the commission. At Forest Hills, the West Side Tennis Club is Tudor, the church is Norman, and some of the houses are Elizabethan.

Atterbury was an unusual architect—he designed country residences, mansions, and millionaires' farms, but also model tenements, hospitals, and low-income housing. With the backing of the Russell Sage Foundation he developed a system for building small, inexpensive houses and designed about forty of them in Forest Hills. Just behind Station Square stands a charming group of fourteen attached houses whose picturesque appearance belies that they are built entirely of precast concrete. Atterbury was interested in prefabrication and invented a nailable concrete called Nailcrete. For Forest Hills, he devised an ingenious building system of hollow concrete floor slabs and wall panels, which were precast in a nearby factory; 140 panels were assembled into a house in only nine days.[33] Even more impressive, since this was the first successful use of precast panel construction in the United States—perhaps in the world—the houses, now almost a hundred years old, are in excellent condition.

I have a choice of two restaurants in the square for lunch. While there is also a beauty shop and a dry cleaner, most of the offices seem to be occupied by real estate companies. "I believe there is money in taste," de Forest had written to Olmsted, and he was proved correct.[34] When Forest Hills opened in 1911, houses sold for $3,000 to $8,000; today, houses regularly sell for more than a million dollars, frequently several million.[35] Three thousand dollars was a lot of money in 1911, and housing reformers such as Lewis Mumford criticized the project because it did not provide housing for blue-collar workers, but—the precast concrete houses apart—that was never the intention.[36] The Russell Sage Foundation wanted to demonstrate that good planning and design could be part of a successful business model, and the high cost of land in Queens meant that houses were targeted at well-off buyers.

Forest Hills was intended to demonstrate "how the thing can be done tastefully and at the same time with due regard for profit."[37] The project, interrupted by the First World War, did not become a model for the suburban expansion of New York City, as de Forest had hoped, but its national influence was significant. Garden City ideas showed up in the design of a number of company towns, or "industrial villages," as they were called: Olmsted planned Kohler in Wisconsin for the plumbing manufacturer; Atterbury laid out two industrial villages, one in Worcester, Massachusetts, the other in Erwin, Tennessee. During the First World War, Olmsted served as manager of a government agency that built housing for war-industry workers, and several of the new suburban worker communities built in 1918—Yorkship Village in Camden, New Jersey; Union Park Gardens in Wilmington, Delaware; and several projects in Bridgeport, Connecticut—clearly owe a debt to Forest Hills. The planner of Union Park Gardens was Olmsted's talented student John Nolen, who went on to plan the garden suburb of Mariemont outside Cincinnati, where Atterbury designed one of the housing groups.

Robert A. M. Stern has described Forest Hills as "both a pinnacle and an end of a particular kind of suburb."[38] After the First World War, railroad suburbs began to be replaced by automobile suburbs, which were less concentrated, and less walkable, than their predecessors, but many of the planning ideas of Forest Hills, such as the seamless fusion of architecture, planning, and landscaping, continued. In addition to the automobile suburb of Mariemont, Nolen planned two full-fledged cities, Kingsport, Tennessee, and Venice, Florida, and the Garden City model influenced real estate developers such as the Van Sweringen brothers at Shaker Heights in Cleveland, Ohio, and Jesse Clyde Nichols at Country Club District in Kansas City, Missouri.[39] Olmsted was responsible for two large garden suburb communities founded during the 1920s: Mountain Lake Club, outside Lake Wales, Florida, and Palos Verdes Estates, south of Los Angeles, the first planned community designed explicitly for private-automobile use. In the late 1920s, planners Clarence Stein and Henry Wright adapted Garden City ideas to Sunnyside Gardens in Queens and Radburn in suburban New Jersey. Their approach was influenced by the then current planning theory that "neighborhood units" should have their own recreation facilities and schools, a concept introduced by planner Clarence Arthur Perry. Perry, who had worked for the Russell Sage Foundation, developed his ideas while living on a shady street in Forest Hills Gardens. Radburn is generally described as an early example of modernist planning, but like all the earlier American garden suburbs, it owes a great debt to the reformist ideas of Ebenezer Howard.

LE CORBUSIER'S TOWERS IN A PARK

Ebenezer Howard was not the only foreigner to influence American cities. Charles-Édouard Jeanneret was born in 1887 in La Chaux-de-Fonds, in the Swiss Jura Mountains. He studied engraving at a local art school (the town was a watchmaking center), but after designing a house when he was only seventeen, he set out to be an architect. Over the next dozen years, he combined apprenticeships with two leading European practitioners—Auguste Perret in Paris and Peter Behrens in Berlin—with architectural travel in Italy, Greece, and Turkey, and a growing domestic practice in Switzerland. At age thirty, feeling constrained by his provincial surroundings, he left La Chaux for Paris.

Architectural commissions were slow in coming. Jeanneret proposed industrial buildings and mass-produced housing prototypes that he hoped would be used in France's post–First World War reconstruction, but none was built, and a concrete-block-manufacturing business venture ended in bankruptcy. Things went slightly better on the artistic front, for the aspiring industrial architect was also a painter. With his friend Amédée Ozenfant, he founded an art movement called Purism. The pair exhibited together, cowrote a manifesto, *Après le Cubisme*, which attacked both Cubism and Futurism, and briefly published a monthly magazine called *L'Esprit Nouveau*—The

New Spirit—which billed itself as an "international review of aesthetics." At this time, Jeanneret adopted the name Le Corbusier for his architectural writing (in part to hide that most of the articles in *L'Esprit Nouveau* were written by its two editors).

Le Corbusier interpreted aesthetics broadly, and his articles dealt with furniture, mass production of houses, transportation, and city planning, as well as architecture. In 1922, he was invited to exhibit in the *urbanisme* section of the Salon d'Automne, an annual avant-garde art and design show that included the likes of Modigliani, Chagall, and Braque. Although Le Corbusier had been asked to contribute "a pretty fountain, or something similar," as he put it, he displayed something much grander: a design for a hypothetical new city.[40] Always immoderate, Le Corbusier covered ninety feet of wall with plans, drawings, and a huge painted diorama. "[My proposal] was greeted with a sort of stupor," he later wrote, "the shock of surprise caused rage in some quarters and enthusiasm in others."[41] Of course, "A Contemporary City of Three Million Inhabitants" (which just happened to be the size of Paris) was intended to shock. The diorama showed a business center consisting of twenty-four identical, sixty-story office buildings—at a time when European cities had no skyscrapers at all and the Eiffel Tower was still the tallest structure in Paris. Equally radical was the absence of traditional streets. The towers were laid out on a widely spaced grid, surrounded by parkland crisscrossed by multilevel roads (trucks below, cars above) and elevated high-speed highways. A large train station stood in the center of the plan, its roof serving as a landing field for commuter aircraft. Residential districts consisting entirely of ten-story apartment blocks, a civic center, and a large park that recalls New York's Central Park completed the plan. The city

was surrounded by a greenbelt, and taking a page from Ebenezer Howard, Le Corbusier included a ring of suburban "garden
cities" on the periphery (during his youthful travels he had lived
in a *Gartenstadte* on the outskirts of Berlin). Although fully two-
thirds of Contemporary City's population was housed in the garden cities, Le Corbusier must have run out of time, for he did
not include details of their design. Nevertheless, the proposal
represented an extraordinary debut for a self-taught city planner
who was basically a penniless Bohemian, living in a seventh-
floor garret in Saint-Germain-des-Prés.*[42]

Le Corbusier's next public foray into city planning occurred
three years later, at the 1925 Exposition Internationale des Arts
Décoratifs et Industriels Modernes. This was a much grander
event, an international trade fair lasting six months and consisting of two hundred pavilions, spread over seventy acres
from the Invalides to the Grand Palais. While many nations
were represented by their top architects (the Austrian pavilion
was designed by Josef Hoffmann, the Belgian pavilion by Victor Horta), the main purpose of the exposition was to promote
French culture and industry. The French designers and architects who took part included up-and-comers such as Eileen
Gray, Pierre Chareau, and Robert Mallet-Stevens, but the stars
of the show were the glamorous Parisian furniture makers and
ensembliers such as Jacques-Émile Ruhlmann, Paul Poiret, and
Maurice Dufrêne. Their stylized geometrical pavilions, exe-
cuted in exotic and lavish materials, gave rise to the style that
would take its name from the exposition—Art Deco.

*Le Corbusier acknowledged the support of Frantz Jourdain, the presi-
dent of the Salon, who apparently paid for mounting the exhibit.

By this time, Le Corbusier had established a small architecture firm (in partnership with his cousin Pierre Jeanneret) and built several villas in and around Paris. He had also achieved a small notoriety with a book, *Vers une architecture,* a collection of his and Ozenfant's *L'Esprit Nouveau* articles. But he was hardly in the same league as Ruhlmann and Poiret, and it is unclear exactly how he got into the exposition. "No funds were available, no site was forthcoming, and the Organizing Committee of the Exhibition refused to allow the scheme I had drawn up to proceed," he later explained in his characteristically melodramatic fashion.[43] Le Corbusier liked to portray himself as a reviled outsider. In fact, his pavilion was sponsored by the motor car company of a famous aeronautical pioneer, Gabriel Voisin, and while the exhibition organizers were distinctly unenthusiastic about his didactic display material, Le Corbusier had the backing of a government minister, Anatole de Monzie, to whom he had been introduced by Gertrude Stein.*[44] In other words, the Swiss architect was a rebel with social connections.

The Pavilion de L'Esprit Nouveau consisted of two parts: a full-size, furnished model apartment, and a city-planning exhibit. Le Corbusier called the large apartment, with two floors and an outdoor roof terrace, an "apartment-villa," since it combined the attributes of a house with high-rise living. The planning exhibit included the material that he had displayed at the Salon d'Automne—drawings, models, a diorama—augmented by an even more radical urban plan. The so-called

*The following year, de Monzie's estranged wife, Gabrielle, and Stein's brother and his wife commissioned a large villa from Le Corbusier, the famous Les Terrasses at Garches.

Voisin Plan applied Le Corbusier's theories to the center of the city of Paris. His proposal covered six hundred acres of the Right Bank, including the Faubourg Saint-Honoré, Les Halles, and the Marais, and called for demolishing all the buildings except for prominent historic landmarks such as the Madeleine, the Opéra, the Palais-Royal, and the Place Vendôme. "Imagine all this junk, which till now has lain spread out over the soil like a dry crust, cleaned off and carted away and replaced by immense clear crystals of glass, rising to a height of over 600 feet," he pronounced.[45] The "junk" was replaced by eighteen sixty-story skyscrapers; as in the earlier plan, highways took the place of streets, and green space surrounded the buildings. "The whole city is a Park," he declared.[46] If anyone thought that "A Contemporary City of Three Million Inhabitants" was merely an intellectual exercise, the Voisin Plan made it clear that its determined creator was deadly serious.

The rather grim little L'Esprit Nouveau pavilion was in an out-of-the-way location at the northernmost extremity of the exposition. Despite its calculated provocations, not the least of which was Le Corbusier's use of distinctly *un*decorative mass-produced objects to furnish the model apartment, the pavilion did not garner much public attention. The *New York Times* article on the fair did not mention it, nor did the lengthy coverage in *Architectural Record*, the leading American professional journal.[47] The official encyclopedia of the exposition cursorily referred to the L'Esprit Nouveau pavilion as merely an "oddity."[48] This lukewarm reception did not discourage Le Corbusier, however, and the Voisin Plan signaled the beginning of two extremely productive decades of city planning. He began by publishing the Voisin Plan and "A Contemporary City of Three

The Voisin Plan remade Paris in a new image.

Million Inhabitants" in a book titled *Urbanisme*. An English translation appeared four years later with the title *The City of Tomorrow*, an obvious reference to *Garden Cities of To-morrow*. Le Corbusier never mentioned Ebenezer Howard, but he was critical of the sort of picturesque planning espoused by Raymond Unwin, which he derided as a "glorification of the curved line and a specious demonstration of its unrivalled beauties."[49]

An important caveat with respect to Le Corbusier's theory of urbanism is that there was not one theory but many. Like Robinson and Howard, the energetic architect was a popularizer and a pamphleteer, but unlike them, he was also an artist. Although *Cartesian* and *rational* were Le Corbusier's favorite words, he was an intuitive thinker who produced urban solutions at the drop of a hat, equally quickly abandoning them—untested—when something else came to mind. Thus, while garden cities played a major role in the Contemporary City proposal, they were roundly denounced in his 1935 urban tract, *La Ville Radieuse* (The Radiant City): "It is necessary to abolish the suburbs and bring nature inside cities."[50] The regular checkerboard of skyscrapers that featured prominently in his first two plans likewise disappeared in later projects. Instead, the buildings grew larger and larger. A plan for a suburb of Rome had four residential towers, each for thirty-four hundred people; a proposal for a new residential district in Barcelona had two mammoth apartment buildings; and a project for Algiers housed the entire commercial district in a single massive skyscraper. This was urbanism reconceived as giant architecture.

The 1930s saw a flurry of master plans. Le Corbusier visited Barcelona, Geneva, Stockholm, Antwerp, and Algiers, made a tour of South America, and en route produced urban makeovers for Montevideo, São Paulo, Buenos Aires, and Rio de Janeiro. Some of these plans were drawn in detail, some were competition entries, but most were merely sketches, made quickly after an afternoon's flyover and a public lecture. Architectural historian Charles Jencks writes of this period, "[Le Corbusier's] output of city plans is remarkable, not only in sheer size, but also in terms of futility. Few were commissioned, fewer still were paid for and perhaps none stood the slightest chance of being adopted."[51] Jencks observes that Le Corbusier's urban writings were at this time increasingly characterized by repetition, bombast, and sloppiness, as if he were in a hurry to put his ideas down on paper. This is especially true of *La Ville Radieuse*, which is a combination of monograph, scrapbook, and hysterical manifesto.

Le Corbusier's unrealized urban visions were unusually

influential. This was partly a result of his unflagging energy: he wrote articles and books, organized exhibitions, lectured widely, and cofounded the Congrès Internationaux d'Architecture Moderne (CIAM), which campaigned for modern city planning. His influence was also the result of his growing reputation as an architect. His practice expanded, and he built several remarkable houses, including the Villa Savoye, which Robert Hughes has called "perhaps the finest example (certainly the most widely published and poetically influential one) of what came to be known as the International Style."[52] In 1927, Le Corbusier was invited to build not one but two houses at an international housing exhibition in Stuttgart, which brought together the leading firebrands of the new architecture, including Mies van der Rohe and Walter Gropius. Le Corbusier was also a finalist in a prominent international competition for the League of Nations headquarters in Geneva. He won a competition to build the Centrosoyuz ministry building in Moscow and was later invited to participate in a competition for the Palace of the Soviets. By then Stalin had turned against modern architecture, and Le Corbusier's design did not win. Nevertheless, the striking proposal cemented its maker's reputation as the leading modernist architect in Europe.

In 1935, Le Corbusier visited the United States at the invitation of New York's Museum of Modern Art, which had included him in its landmark Modern Architecture show three years earlier and was preparing a one-man exhibition of his work. New York, which Le Corbusier termed the "City of the Incredible Towers," impressed him; after all, it was the first time that the creator of the Voisin Plan had actually seen a skyscraper. That did not stop him from pontificating. The day after his arrival

Le Corbusier with a model
of his Radiant City, c. 1930.

he told the *New York Herald Tribune* that he thought Manhattan's skyscrapers were too small and too close together, and that he did not like the "deplorably romantic city ordinance" that mandated setbacks. He spent two and a half months in the United States on a twenty-city lecture tour that took him to all the major universities and colleges of the Northeast and Midwest. Wherever he went, he talked about urbanism, illustrating his public lectures with on-the-spot drawings done with colored crayons on huge sheets of paper. His ideas were well received by his young audiences. Since the skyscraper was an American invention, the concept of vertical cities was familiar; Americans had the highest rate of car ownership in the world, so the notion of a city planned to favor driving made sense—more sense than in Europe, where the private car was still a luxury; and American downtowns, unlike their European counterparts, had always been commercial centers, so the separation of uses—a key ingredient of the Radiant City concept—was familiar, too.

Although Le Corbusier was hoping for American commissions, none was forthcoming. But his influence was felt in the immensely popular Futurama exhibit at the New York World's Fair of 1939. Created by the industrial designer Norman Bel Geddes, the display represented the United States twenty years hence. Visitors were transported above a vast model in suspended seats, like a horizontal ski chairlift, which gave the illusion of flying over the continent, coast to coast.[53] The model showed an urbanized landscape that included cities with extremely tall skyscrapers, elevated walkways, and underground parking garages. This was in many ways an adaptation of the Voisin Plan, but Bel Geddes's vision of the urban future was far more expansive than Le Corbusier's, and the cities in Futurama were surrounded by sprawling suburban communities, connected to one another by a network of superhighways. Since the exhibit was part of the General Motors pavilion, the model was equipped with thousands of tiny moving cars.

On leaving Futurama each visitor received a blue-and-white lapel button reading I HAVE SEEN THE FUTURE. It didn't take twenty years for the future to arrive, however. Only four years after the World's Fair closed, the Metropolitan Life Insurance Company, encouraged by Robert Moses, started to build a series of unusual residential projects in New York City. Parkchester, Stuyvesant Town, and Peter Cooper Village have often been described as American versions of the Radiant City.[54] Stuyvesant Town, for example, designed in 1943 by a team led by Richmond H. Shreve, consolidated eighteen city blocks into one large parcel, housing twenty-four thousand people in thirty-five more or less identical apartment blocks. The spaces between the buildings included parks and playgrounds, as well as parking lots.

Equally influential as its parklike setting was the Radiant City's separation of urban functions. Major American cities such as Los Angeles and New York had adopted zoning legislation before the First World War, but Le Corbusier gave zoning an aesthetic rationale. Henceforth, not only would residential and commercial uses be placed apart, but a variety of other functions would be isolated in self-sufficient "centers"—shopping centers, convention centers, cultural centers, government centers, sports centers, and so on. The modern city would no longer be a hodgepodge of activities; it would be ordered, logical, *planned*.

Le Corbusier died in 1965, in the middle of a decade that saw his urban vision realized around the world: in Europe, in South America, where his disciples built the new city of Brasília, and in India, where he designed the master plan for the city of Chandigarh. The Soviet Union, which had rejected his architecture in the 1920s, adopted his ideas of mass-produced housing and high-rise urbanism and exported them to its ally Communist China. In America, the designers of the public housing projects that were built in almost every major city also adopted Le Corbusier's vision. The largest of the so-called projects, Robert Taylor Homes in Chicago, designed in 1962 by the city's leading modernist firm, Skidmore, Owings & Merrill, consisted of twenty-eight identical apartment slabs lined up in lockstep precision on a two-mile-long superblock.

Only forty years had passed since Le Corbusier unveiled

"A Contemporary City of Three Million Inhabitants" at the Salon d'Automne. Nothing would appear less likely than that urban theories dreamed up in a Parisian garret would take hold in America, but that is exactly what happened. By the late 1950s, the City Beautiful and Garden City movements were a distant memory, the giants of that period either dead, such as Nolen and Atterbury, or retired, such as Olmsted Jr. Forest Hills Gardens was only a few decades old, but to the new generation of architects and planners it already seemed stodgy and old-fashioned, especially when compared to the exciting novelty of the Radiant City.

3

Home Remedies

Throughout the 1950s the ideas typified by the Radiant City reigned supreme. That they were eventually called into question is due in no small part to the influence of a single person, Jane Jacobs, who must be accorded equal footing with Charles Mulford Robinson, Ebenezer Howard, and Le Corbusier as a seminal figure in twentieth-century American urbanism. Unlike Le Corbusier, Jacobs was neither an architect nor a city planner; like Robinson, she was a journalist, writer, and activist; and like Howard—with whom she would vociferously disagree—she was largely self-taught. She was born Jane Butzner, in 1916 in Scranton, Pennsylvania, a doctor's daughter. After graduating from high school and taking a secretarial course, she left the declining coal-mining city for New York. It was the middle of the Depression, and she found work as a stenographer, and later as a freelance magazine writer; during the war, she was employed by the U.S. Office of War Information and the State Department. She married Robert Jacobs, an architect, and in 1952, inspired by reading a magazine to which he subscribed, she applied for and got a job as an associate editor at *Architectural Forum*.

Architectural Forum was owned by Time Inc., which at the time was the most prestigious magazine publisher in the United States, perhaps in the world. Time's founder, Henry Luce, who was interested in design and urbanism, had bought *Architectural Forum* in 1932 and turned it into the liveliest architectural periodical in the country (his financial support was crucial, since *Forum* never turned a profit). Jacobs was initially hired to write about hospitals and schools, but increasingly covered urban issues.[1] Unlike architectural periodicals today, which consist chiefly of photographs, *Architectural Forum* included long articles on a wide range of topical issues. Jacobs's reporting took her to different cities—Philadelphia, Washington, D.C., Saint Louis, Fort Worth—where she visited urban redevelopment projects and interviewed planning officials.

In 1956, the editor of the magazine, Douglas Haskell, was invited by Harvard's Graduate School of Design to speak at a conference on urban planning, but since he was on vacation, he sent Jacobs in his stead. She chose an unlikely subject for her ten-minute talk: the lack of stores in urban redevelopment projects. She described traditional shopping streets as "strips of chaos that have a weird wisdom of their own not yet encompassed in our concept of urban order." She made the point that shopkeepers were important "public characters," that corner stores functioned not just as shops but as neighborhood social centers, and that even vacant stores played a role as storefront clubs and meeting places. The new housing projects, with their massive residential slabs set in parkland, provided no such options. "This is a ludicrous situation, and it ought to give planners the shivers," she said. She talked about how the chief social space of the inhabitants of a new housing project in East Harlem (where she served as a board member of Union Settlement) was a laundry room. "We wonder if the planner of that project had any idea its heart would be in the basement," she observed caustically. "And we wonder if the architect had any idea what he was designing when he did that laundry."[2] Jacobs, lacking academic credentials, based her arguments on simple observation, but her conclusions were an unvarnished condemnation of architecture and city planning. Lewis Mumford, who was at the conference, later described the scene: "Into the foggy atmosphere of professional jargon that usually envelops such meetings, she blew like a fresh, off-shore breeze to present a picture, dramatic but not distorted, of the results of displacing large neighborhood populations to facilitate large-scale rebuilding."[3]

Another participant in the Harvard conference who was impressed by Jacobs's talk was William H. Whyte Jr., assistant managing editor of Time Inc.'s flagship business magazine, *Fortune*. "Holly" Whyte, whose bestselling book, *The Organization Man*, appeared that year, was a longtime student of cities who would write several influential books on city design, including *The Last Landscape* (1968), *The Social Life of Small Urban Spaces* (1980), and *City* (1988). He shared Jacobs's skepticism about urban redevelopment, and he invited her to contribute to a forthcoming series in *Fortune* on the American metropolis. Although Jacobs at first demurred—Whyte's colleagues were distinctly unenthusiastic, seeing her as an interloper—she eventually agreed.[4]

The series began in September 1957 with an essay by Whyte provocatively titled "Are Cities Un-American?" He argued that after several decades of neglect American cities faced many challenges, not only physical decay and poverty, but also a loss of population to the suburbs, whose rapid growth was evidence of the middle class's growing disaffection with city life. The 1948 Urban Renewal Act provided federal support to municipal governments to clear slum areas and sell the land to private developers. Like Jacobs, Whyte was not impressed with the results. "In the plans for the huge redevelopment projects to come, we are being shown a new image of the city—and it is sterile and lifeless," he wrote, referring to the designs of architects firmly in thrall to the Radiant City. For Whyte, the key issue was "Will the city assert itself as a good place to *live*?"[5]

To answer this question, Whyte enlisted the considerable resources of Time Inc., contacting correspondents in various cities, commissioning national polls and opinion surveys, and convening panels of experts. His own article, for example, was accompanied by a preference survey of upper-income apartment dwellers, which highlighted the differences between high-rise and low-rise urban living and identified many downtown residents as what would today be called empty nesters, that is, older couples who had moved back to the city from the suburbs. Whyte's article was illustrated with views of typical residential streets in a variety of American cities: Columbia Heights in Brooklyn, Russian Hill in San Francisco, shotgun houses in New Orleans. The Utrillo-like drawings, by Orfeo Tamburi, a Paris-based artist, reminded readers that American cities, no less than their European counterparts, have a tradition of urban living. Subsequent articles in the series, written by *Fortune* editors Francis Bello, Seymour Freedgood, and Daniel Seligman, as well as Whyte, covered transportation, city administration, slums, and urban sprawl. The reports are striking for their intelligence, detail, length—and sense of urgency. The common message was that American cities had a unique opportunity to renew themselves, but they had to get it right.

Jacobs's article was the last in the six-part series, though not by design. *Fortune*'s publisher, C. D. Jackson, found her draft too controversial, causing a two-month delay while he, Whyte, and Jacobs argued back and forth.[6] The article finally appeared in the April 1958 issue. "Downtown Is for People" was a scathing indictment of urban renewal. "What will the projects look like?" Jacobs asked. "They will be spacious, park-like, and uncrowded. They will feature long green vistas. They will be stable and symmetrical and orderly. They will be clean, impressive, and monumental. They will have all the attributes of a well-kept, dignified cemetery."[7] She singled out several redevelopment schemes for particular criticism: the underground concourses of Penn Center in Philadelphia; a suburban-style shopping mall in downtown Pittsburgh; the cultural superblock of Lincoln Center in New York (the target that had upset Jackson). The thrust of her argument was that while cities needed improvement, rebuilding should safeguard and reinforce traditional urban attributes, especially lively streets. The previous *Fortune* authors depended on surveys and round-tables of experts, but Jacobs relied on her own observations at ground level—sidewalk level—to appreciate how people actually behaved on city streets. She extolled density, complexity, and diversity and pointed out the advantages of narrow streets, short blocks, mixtures of old and new buildings, and mixtures of commercial, cultural, and residential uses. "Designing a dream city is easy," she wrote, implicitly criticizing the urban visions of architects and planners, "rebuilding a living city takes imagination."[8] Jacobs saw urban rebuilding as piecemeal, governed less by professionals than by citizens, a foreshadowing of the community groups, review boards, and business groups that would, in fact, later play a major role in shaping city development.

The *Fortune* series was published as a book, *The Exploding Metropolis: A Study of the Assault on Urbanism and How Our Cities Can Resist It*, which was favorably reviewed by Harrison Salisbury on the front page of the *New York Times Book Review*.[9] The book's editor, Nathan Glazer, was a thirty-four-year-old sociologist and coauthor of the influential book *The Lonely Crowd*. After meeting Glazer, Jacobs invited him to write an article about urbanism for *Architectural Forum*. The result, "Why City Planning Is Obsolete," would influence Jacobs's thinking. In the article, Glazer points out that the profession of city planning, rooted in the Garden City ideas of Ebenezer Howard, is ill suited to deal with the problems of large cities. "What passes for city planning today is fundamentally a rejection of the big city and of all it means—its variety, its peculiarities, its richness of choice and experience—and a yearning for a bucolic society," he writes.[10] Glazer makes the original observation that while in many ways Le Corbusier's Radiant City was diametrically opposed to Howard's Garden City—being vertical rather than horizontal—the two concepts shared a common assumption, "that the city could be improved by replacing its chaos and confusion with a single plan, different from the urban plans of the past in that it was not conceived as a general outline of streets and major public institutions, but as a place-ment of every residence, every facility, every plot of green."[11]

Glazer argued that current American city planning was a fusion of Howard's and Le Corbusier's ideas, and he criticized the suburban character of such well-known projects as Louis I. Kahn's Mill Creek housing in Philadelphia and Mies van der Rohe's Lafayette Park in Detroit, which combined apartment towers and freestanding groups of row houses in parklike set-tings. Glazer's chief point was that big cities are not only larger and denser than suburbs and towns, but are actually different, experientially richer and culturally and economically more diverse. What was needed, he wrote, were planning concepts that would create and preserve "the character of a city rather than that of a suburb or a town."[12] He disagreed with the sugges-tion that a disinterested party—the planner—could do a better job organizing the city than a multitude of self-interested indi-viduals as represented by the market. He argued that individual decisions were responsible for the liveliness and variety of cities. Anticipating the historic preservation movement, Glazer also called for saving old buildings and old neighborhoods.

When Jacobs was approached by the Rockefeller Foundation with an offer of a grant if she would expand her *Fortune* essay into a book, Glazer introduced her to Jason Epstein at Random House.[13] The result was *The Death and Life of Great American Cities*. The book elaborated on the various themes Jacobs had broached in her *Fortune* essay, her Harvard talk, and her *Archi-tectural Forum* articles. She used examples chiefly from Green-wich Village (where she lived) and also described older city neighborhoods such as Back-of-the-Yards in Chicago and the North End in Boston, as well as developments she had visited in Philadelphia, Pittsburgh, and Baltimore. As before, she pinpointed busy streets as the key ingredient for successful urban neighborhoods, but to the attributes of liveliness and human interest she added public safety, a theme that runs throughout the book. *Death and Life* is a forcefully argued, jargon-free book aimed at a wide audience that benefits from Jacobs's twenty years of practicing journalism — and twenty years of walking the streets of New York City.

Jacobs's *Fortune* article had included a single disparaging reference to the "dated relics" of the City Beautiful movement, but otherwise had little to say about city planning. Not so *Death and Life*, whose first lines lay out the author's position with characteristic bluntness:

> This book is an attack on current city planning and rebuilding. It is also, and mostly, an attempt to introduce new principles of city planning and rebuilding, different and even opposite from those now taught in everything from schools of architecture and planning to the Sunday supplements and women's magazines. My attack is not based on quibbles about rebuilding methods or hair-splitting about fashions in design. It is an attack, rather, on the principles and aims that have shaped modern, orthodox city planning and rebuilding.[14]

Jacobs's provocative position was influenced by Glazer's *Architectural Forum* article, but she went further, lumping the three Big Ideas together and sarcastically referring to them as "Radiant Garden City Beautiful." She dismissed the achievements of the City Beautiful movement such as Philadelphia's Benjamin Franklin Parkway, and San Francisco's Civic Center,

Jane Jacobs in 1962,
the year after she published *The Death
and Life of Great American Cities.*

pointing out that not only did people tend to avoid these monumental spaces, but their effect on the city was generally negative rather than uplifting. Referring to the World's Columbian Exposition, she wrote, "Somehow, when the fair became part of the city, it did not work like the fair."[15] She had nothing good to say about garden cities, either. "[Ebenezer Howard] simply wrote off the intricate, many-faceted, cultural life of the metropolis. He was uninterested in such problems as the way great cities police themselves, or exchange ideas, or operate politically, or invent new economic arrangements," she wrote.[16] She criticized not only Howard and Unwin, but also American proponents of regional planning and urban decentralization such as Mumford, Stein, and Wright, and the housing expert Catherine Bauer. She reserved her greatest scorn for Le Corbusier and the Radiant City. "His city was like a wonderful mechanical toy," she wrote. "It was so orderly, so visible, so easy to understand. It said everything in a flash, like a good advertisement."[17] She excoriated the notion of eliminating streets. "The whole idea of doing away with city streets, insofar as that is possible, and downgrading and minimizing their social and their economic part in city life is the most mischievous and destructive idea in orthodox city planning."[18]

Like Glazer, Jacobs objected to modern city planning on pragmatic grounds. "Cities are an immense laboratory of trial and error, failure and success, in city building and city design," she wrote. Why couldn't city planners learn from these experiments? She felt that practitioners and students of planning should study the successes and failures of actual living cities, not historic examples and theoretical projects. She adamantly opposed what she called "architectural design cults," which is how she characterized the City Beautiful and the Radiant City. She attacked a key assumption of modern planning: "A city cannot be a work of art. When we deal with cities we are dealing with life at its most complex and intense. Because this is so, there is a basic esthetic limitation on what can be done with cities."[19] She did not mean that beauty could not be a part of the experience of a city, but she was criticizing the diagrammatic plans made by architects, and the tendency of large projects to sanitize the urban environment, resulting in places that seemed to her entirely divorced from the "messy" nature of city life.

The Death and Life of Great American Cities was published in November 1961, to great acclaim. Excerpts appeared in *Harp-*

er's, the *Saturday Evening Post*, and *Vogue*, and the book was widely reviewed, with the popular press generally liking it, and professional journals expressing a degree of skepticism. Yet everyone recognized the book's importance. Lloyd Rodwin, an MIT city planner writing in the *New York Times Book Review*, took exception to some of Jacobs's criticisms of his profession, but called *Death and Life* "a great book."[20] City planners might have been expected to react more strongly to Jacobs's attack, but most didn't. Perhaps they were disarmed by her commonsense observations, perhaps they secretly agreed with her conclusions, or perhaps they were simply glad to see the subject of city planning in the public eye, no matter the message.

Death and Life was a finalist for the 1962 nonfiction National Book Award, which went to another book on urbanism, *The City in History*, by Lewis Mumford. Mumford, sixty-seven, had long been active as a literary critic, essayist, historian of technology, urban reformer, and architecture critic. Since 1931, his "Sky Line" column in the *New Yorker* had provided a national platform for his ideas about urbanism, and thanks to *The Culture of Cities* (1938), and now *The City in History*, he was widely recognized as America's leading thinker and writer on the subject. Like Jacobs, Mumford opposed Le Corbusier's Radiant City, but he had long been an advocate for Garden City planning, so he might have been expected to respond publicly to her book. Respond he did, a year later, in a scathing *New Yorker* review sarcastically titled "Mother Jacobs' Home Remedies."

Mumford's negative reaction to *Death and Life* was partly the result of pique. He had befriended Jacobs, corresponded with her, and encouraged her book writing, and she reciprocated by ridiculing the work of men he admired and calling *The Culture*

Witold Rybczynski

Lewis Mumford, whose views
on urbanism clashed with
those of Jane Jacobs.

of Cities "a morbid and biased catalog of ills."[21] The differences
between Mumford and Jacobs were substantive. He shared her
views about the complexity of cities and the need to avoid sim-
plistic solutions, but took issue with many of her sweeping gen-
eralizations. For example, in the review he disagreed with her
blanket condemnation of urban parks as dangerous; a native
New Yorker, Mumford was old enough to remember when
Central Park had been perfectly safe (as it would again be by the
late 1980s). He also took issue with her claim that high-density
housing, pedestrian-filled streets, and a mixture of economic
activities were sufficient to combat crime and violence, pointing out that Harlem, then New York's least safe neighborhood,

had all three conditions to no avail. He questioned her acerbic characterization of suburbia. "It is millions of quite ordinary people who cherish such suburban desires, not a few fanatical haters of the city, sunk in bucolic dreams," he wrote.[22] He also violently disagreed with her claim that cities do not involve artistry. "What has happened is that Mrs. Jacobs has jumped from the quite defensible position that good physical structures and handsome design are not everything in city planning to the callow notion that they do not matter at all."[23]

Although Mumford conceded that Jacobs was a perceptive observer of urban life—"no one has surpassed her in understanding the reasons for the great metropolis's complexity"—he was irked by her categorical rejection of city planning.[24] He had a lifelong commitment to planning, having personally known the great Scottish pioneer of city planning, Sir Patrick Geddes, who laid the foundation for the city-planning profession, just as Olmsted had for landscape architecture. A supporter of the Garden City movement, Geddes (1854–1932) expanded Howard's ideas to include the urban region and, trained as a biologist and botanist, was an early advocate of ecology and nature conservation. His influence was far-ranging and included on not only Unwin and Nolen, but even Le Corbusier. In 1923, to advance Geddes's ideas in the United States, Mumford, Stein, and other urban reformers founded the Regional Planning Association of America, which promoted developments such as Radburn, New Jersey, and Sunnyside Gardens in New York City. Thus, many of the planned communities that Jacobs criticized were projects that Mumford had personally supported. For ten years, he had lived in Stein and Wright's Sunnyside Gardens. "Not utopia," he observed, "but better than any existing New York neighborhood, even Mrs. Jacobs' backwater in Greenwich Village."[25]

Mumford characterized *Death and Life* as "a mingling of sense and sentimentality, of mature judgments and schoolgirl howlers."[26] That may have been unkind, but it was not entirely untrue. Jacobs was trained as a journalist, not a scholar, and she tended to dramatize and exaggerate for effect, picking and choosing evidence to support her arguments. Her knowledge of urban history was limited. She did not recognize, for example, that the City Beautiful movement was not only about monumental civic centers and parkways, but also about piecemeal improvement. Her potted chronicle of the influence of the Garden City movement in America simply skipped over the fecund pre–Second World War era, and she seemed unaware of Burnham's Chicago Plan, with its comprehensive descriptions of a rich and varied city life, or of developments such as Forest Hills Gardens, which, with its mixture of uses and its density, was close to what she espoused. She also tended to draw large conclusions from small examples, citing high 1958 crime rates in Los Angeles as proof that automobile-oriented cities are inherently dangerous, which is a dubious proposition, as the future would show, for crime rates in pedestrian-oriented cities such as Baltimore, Saint Louis, and New York City would soon soar. Her analysis of urban decline was likewise flawed. Cities were not in trouble because of poor planning, but because, since before the First World War, the middle class had been decamping for the suburbs, leaving behind poverty, rising crime, and racial tensions and abandoning precisely those dense downtown neighborhoods that she extolled.

That Jacobs was neither a sociologist nor an urban historian is a weakness of her book, but also its strength. She approached her subject quite differently from professional planners; instead of formulating a theory of what cities should be, she tried to understand what they actually were, and how they worked—and didn't work. As a result, where planners saw confusion, she discovered an intricate web of human relationships; where they perceived messy chaos, she found vitality and liveliness. She rejected planners' attempts to define cities as simple structures, whether biological or technological, and instead offered her own striking analogy: the city as a field of darkness.

> In the field, many fires are burning. They are of many sizes, some great, others small; some far apart, others dotted close together; some are brightening, some are slowly going out. Each fire, large or small, extends its radiance into the surrounding murk, and thus it carves out a space. But the space and the shape of that space exist only to the extent that the light from the fire creates it.
>
> The murk has no shape or pattern except where it is carved into space by the light. Where the murk between the lights becomes deep and undefinable and shapeless, the only way to give it form or structure is to kindle new fires in the murk or sufficiently enlarge the nearest existing fire.[27]

Jacobs considered cities not to be "simple problems" that could be solved with one-dimensional solutions, such as separating pedestrians from cars, or putting everyone in tall buildings, or building parks. Nor were cities so chaotic that they required radical reorganization, such as isolating housing, commerce, and industry though zoning. She described cities as "complex problems" in which dozens of variables are subtly organized into an interconnected whole. "Their intricate order—a manifestation of the freedom of countless numbers of people to make and carry out countless plans—is in many ways a great wonder," she concluded.[28]

4

Mr. Wright and
the Disappearing City

Frank Lloyd Wright is not mentioned in *The Death and Life of Great American Cities,* but his influence on American urbanism was at least as important as that of the Radiant Garden City Beautiful. Wright first broached the subject of urbanism in the late spring of 1930, when he was invited to deliver the Kahn Lectures at Princeton University. After five lectures that covered architecture, technology, style, housing, and skyscrapers, he devoted the final talk to "The City." What he said would have surprised his audience. "I believe the city as we know it today, is to die," he asserted, listing the various technologies—airplanes, automobiles, telephones, radio—that were encouraging people to spread out.[1] He anticipated the impact of television, although it was then in its infancy. "The 'movies,' 'talkies' and all, will soon be seen and heard better at home than in any hall. Symphony concerts, operas and lectures will eventually be taken more easily to the home than the people there can be taken to the great halls in old style, and be heard more satisfactorily in congenial company. The home of the individual social unit will contain in itself in this respect all the city heretofore could afford, plus intimate comfort and free individual choice."[2] Wright did not provide any specific details of what would replace the traditional city, but he was adamant about one thing: the future would in no way resemble "Le Corbusier and his school."[3]

Not long after, Wright confronted Le Corbusier's ideas head-on. On January 3, 1932, the *New York Times Magazine* published a critique of American urbanism under the heading "A Noted Architect Dissects Our Cities"—the author was Le Corbusier. While conceding that the United States was leading the world in modern technology, and despite never having set foot in an American city (his first visit occurred three years later), Le Corbusier was unbending in his judgment: "I absolutely refuse to admit, nevertheless, as many so lightly do, that Manhattan and Chicago possess the architecture and town planning of modern times. No, and again no!"[4] The article was illustrated with an aerial view of the Voisin Plan and preached the virtues of tall buildings surrounded by greenery. His views on suburbs had hardened. "This new city will be the reverse of the garden city, fundamentally opposed to it in principle. Since the garden city is situated in the suburbs and so extends the area of the town, it creates a transport problem, but as the green city will reduce the town area this problem will be done away with entirely." In case there was any doubt, he added, "We must immediately discard the traditional type of house."[5] Since the majority of Americans lived in single-family houses—in cities as well as suburbs—this was a calculated provocation.

Less than three months later, the *New York Times Magazine* published Wright's response under the headline "Broadacre City: An Architect's Vision." It is unclear whether Wright was invited to write the article, or whether, as he often did with the press, he volunteered. Probably the latter, for he was irritated by the attention being lavished on European architects. A month earlier, the Museum of Modern Art had opened its Modern Architecture exhibition, and although Wright's work was included, the focus was firmly on the work of the European modernists, whose work the exhibition's organizers christened the International Style.[6] The *New York Times* article was a chance for Wright to regain the limelight.

Wright had favorably reviewed the English translation of *Vers une architecture* four years earlier, but his *Times* essay is a spirited point-by-point rebuttal of Le Corbusier's urban theories.[7] Wright reiterates his view that the concentrated city has been rendered obsolete by modern technologies such as the automobile and telecommunications. People can spread out—they no longer need to live in dense concentrations. "Centralization by way of the city has had a big day and a long day. It is not dead yet. But it is no longer a necessity or a luxury," he writes. "And 1,000 people to the hectare [a reference to the urban density that Le Corbusier proposed in his article] . . . is 980 too many."[8] While Le Corbusier wanted to bring nature into the city in the form of parks, Wright suggests the exact opposite; take the city into the countryside, he advises. Expanding his Princeton lecture, he describes people shopping in roadside markets, working on farms and in factories, and living in individual houses that are spread out over the landscape and linked by a network of highways. Wright was vague about the details of this decentralized city and included no plans or drawings, but he did give it a name: Broadacre City.*

Where did Broadacre City come from? Wright was sixty-five when he wrote the *New York Times* article, fully twenty years older than Le Corbusier. He belonged to an earlier generation and had the reputation of being a romantic, yet his ideas about urbanism, unlike those of the European architect, were grounded in direct observation. While Le Corbusier had been living in Paris dreaming about cities of skyscrapers, Wright had been experiencing his vision of urbanism firsthand—in Los Angeles. In the early 1920s, he spent several years living and working in the city, which was then one of the fastest-growing cities in the country, and growing in ways that made it different from any other city in the world. Though not particularly large in terms of population—about half a million—the city was spread over seventy miles. For Wright, who had previously lived in the dense Chicago suburbs, and who loved driving, cruising the boulevards and drives of Los Angeles was an eye-opener.

The public exchange with Le Corbusier stimulated Wright to publish a short book titled *The Disappearing City.*[9] In it he elaborated on the themes of his Princeton lecture and *Times* article and elucidated a key principle: "We are going to call this city for the individual the Broadacre City because it is based upon a minimum of an acre to the family."[10] In Wright's scheme, which was influenced by the theories of the maverick economist Henry George, each individual would receive an

---

*The *New York Times* article was misleadingly illustrated by a drawing of a high-rise apartment building, Wright's Saint Mark's-in-the-Bouwerie proposal for New York City.

acre of land in a vast redistribution scheme, "opening the way for him to be a better citizen in a better country."[11] Although *The Disappearing City* did not include any plans, Wright provided detailed written descriptions of Broadacre City, in many cases referring to his earlier designs for apartment buildings, hotels, and houses. Catherine Bauer, a planner and housing advocate writing in the *Nation,* found his proposal to be Utopian and impractical.[12] The *New York Times Book Review,* however, was more positive: "Economists are already looking around for the industry which will lift us out of the depression. Housing in urban regions seems a poor agent for this task because of the high cost of land and the existence of 'dead areas' and what might be called dead buildings. But housing on land which is cheap because it is outside the cities, carried out by methods and materials which technology already has at its command, might be a different story. One would like to see architects of Mr. Wright's social view point entrusted with such an experiment."[13]

During the winter of 1934–35, Wright, with the financial support of Edgar J. Kaufmann, a Pittsburgh department-store magnate for whom he was designing a weekend house (the soon-to-be-famous Fallingwater), gave Broadacre City physical form. As Le Corbusier had done with "A Contemporary City of Three Million Inhabitants," Wright imagined a hypothetical site: four square miles of vaguely Midwestern topography including farmland, a portion of a river, and a section of hillside. Following Midwestern custom, a grid of roads divides the land into quarter sections; some of the roads are two-level highways, cars above and trucks below, with specially designed interchanges (limited-access highways were still a novelty).

There is no functional zoning; instead, schools, civic buildings, factories, a county seat, and an arena are scattered among orchards, vineyards, farms, and recreational spaces. People live in houses on acre lots, as well as in apartment towers and on small farms. Wright's idea of a substitute for the traditional city is much more radical than Le Corbusier's proposal and differs from it in two important respects. First, there is no center or commercial core, nothing that resembles a traditional downtown, no architectural focus at all. Second, Wright's plan does not represent a complete city; it is merely a small portion of an urban pattern that can go on forever. Since the four square miles represented by the plan would have housed a population of only seven thousand, to accommodate 3 million people would have required seventeen hundred square miles, that is, thirty times the area of Le Corbusier's Contemporary City, but smaller than metropolitan Seattle, which has a comparable population spread over 5,894 square miles.*

Broadacre City was unveiled to the public in 1935 at the monthlong Industrial Arts Exposition held in New York's Rockefeller Center. The display included plans and drawings and a giant twelve-foot-square model. Wright continued to tinker with this model for the next two and a half decades and published two more books on Broadacre City: in 1945, *When Democracy Builds*, a further elaboration of *The Disappearing City*; and the year before he died, *The Living City*. The latter is heavily illustrated with drawings and models of buildings: prefabricated

---

*Le Corbusier's Contemporary City included unbuilt open areas of greenbelt. The gross density of Broadacre City was 1,750 people per square mile (compared to the average gross suburban density today, which is 2,149 people per square mile).

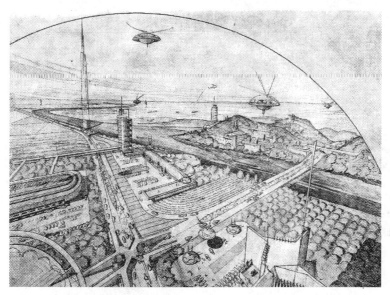

Broadacre City was a vision of a highly decentralized urban future, with private flying machines and strip malls.

houses, fireproof farmhouses, schools, and service stations. Despite futuristic touches such as flying-saucer-like helicopter taxis and odd-looking cars of his own design, Wright insists that his vision of the future is not Utopian. "There is plenty of evidence now at hand to substantiate all the changes I outline," he writes in a section titled "Democracy in Overalls."[14]

Except for a couple of small subdivisions, Wright never built even a small version of Broadacre City, and neither did anyone else for, unlike the City Beautiful and the Garden City, Broadacre City did not spawn a movement. Wright was too little the organizer, and too much the individualist, for that. Another problem was that admirers of his architecture, who were legion, generally found his urban vision unpalatable, if not downright embarrassing. "One cannot but give pause to a few questions which suggest themselves," wrote a reviewer of *The Disappearing City.* "Would so complete a lack of community organization be amenable to the inhabitants? Is not man naturally a gregarious animal? What will become of the beauty of the countryside, once it becomes webbed with giant highways and flecked with super–filling stations?"[15] Mumford was likewise skeptical: "Frank Lloyd Wright's scheme for Broadacre City, in which each family would have a minimum of one acre of land, limits social intercourse on the primary level to a mere handful of neighbors and above that level demands motor transportation for even the most casual or ephemeral meetings."[16]

Although Wright never built a version of Broadacre City, as architectural historian David De Long observes, everything that the architect designed in his later years can be seen as contributing toward his urban vision. Wright populated the great model with tiny examples of his own buildings, "each a demonstration of principle, each conceived to uphold his ideal of organic architecture, each meant to sustain a sense of individual freedom, each shaped to enhance human life through meaningful connection, each conceived as a visible part of a universal order," De Long writes.[17]

One aspect of the Broadacre idea that Wright did realize was the individual family house. In 1936, shortly after he unveiled the model of his proposed city, Wright began building the first in a series of houses that he called Usonians, the sort of small, affordable homes that were the staple of Broadacre City. He published the designs in popular magazines such as *House and Home* and *House Beautiful,* and the houses' distinctive features—one-story

Frank Lloyd Wright
at eighty-four.

layouts, low roofs, carports, kitchens overlooking living areas, and rough stone fireplaces—soon showed up in so-called ranch houses built by ordinary builders. Between 1935 and his death in 1959, Wright built more than 150 Usonians, and his idea of living in houses in a countrylike setting, which is, after all, the mainstay of Broadacre City, took hold in the American popular imagination.

Wright's much derided vision of a decentralized American urbanism turned into reality as more and more middle-class— and increasingly, working-class—families moved to the suburbs. Moreover, all the new postwar Sunbelt cities, such as Atlanta, Houston, and Phoenix, followed a Broadacre pattern—spreading out rather than going up. Many factors accelerated this dispersal. In marked contrast to urban renewal, ranch houses and residential subdivisions proved both popular and successful.

The 1956 Federal-Aid Highway Act, which funded the interstate highway system, opened up outlying rural areas to urbanization. That same year saw the construction of the first fully enclosed shopping mall, not so different from the glass-roofed "roadside markets" of Broadacre City, supporting Wright's contention that "ideas always precede and prefigure facts."[18]

The ascendancy of automobile travel took place just as Wright foretold. In fact, the technological forces fueling decentralization proved even more numerous than he imagined. Growth outside the cities has been accelerated by cheap and ubiquitous air travel (which he foresaw), and cable television, home videos, cell phones, and the Internet (which he didn't). Not only enclosed shopping malls but a variety of other suburban building types such as megachurches, office parks, gas-stations-cum-convenience-stores, and suburban high-rises eerily fulfilled his original vision. Wright, despite his eccentricities, had an uncanny sense of the likes and dislikes of his fellow citizens. Americans do prefer freestanding houses to apartments, and "one acre per family," which seemed a far-fetched formula in the 1930s, has turned out to be not far off the mark, although the acre tends to be planted in lawn rather than corn. Of course, banal shopping strips and gated communities are not what Wright had in mind, but they are, in many ways, a logical extension of his decentralizing vision.

Wright was mistaken about one thing, however: the city hasn't disappeared. Even as metropolitan areas have spread out in crude versions of Broadacre City, the centers of most cities have also grown, and while older industrial centers such as Detroit, Baltimore, and Cleveland have faltered, New York, Boston, and San Francisco have found new life. But perhaps

Wright never completely believed his own dire prognostication. At the same time as he was writing *The Living City,* he proposed a 528-story state office building for Chicago's lakefront called the Mile High Illinois. "No one can afford to build it now," he announced when he unveiled his design, "but in the future no one can afford *not* to build it."[19] He was right about that, too. Downtown Chicago would grow vertically by leaps and bounds, first the John Hancock Building, then the Sears Tower, and in 2005 a Chicago developer proposed a 115-story skyscraper. That project has been abandoned, but a half-mile-high skyscraper—currently the tallest structure in the world—has gone up in Dubai. The stalagmite shape of the Burj Khalifa, designed by the Chicago office of Skidmore, Owings & Merrill, recalls the Mile High design. And it is, of course, in a city.

5

The Demand-Side
of Urbanism

Postwar suburban growth was influenced by Frank Lloyd Wright
and Broadacre City, but suburbanization was accelerated by the
urban riots of the "long hot summers" of the mid-1960s. Los
Angeles, Cleveland, San Francisco, Newark, Detroit, Boston, as
well as Harlem and Bedford-Stuyvesant in New York, suffered
arson, looting, and civil unrest. In the decade that followed,
urban crime rates soared, businesses moved out of downtown,
and city populations continued to shrink. The old cities of the
Northeast were also affected by a major national demographic
move to the Sunbelt. As political analyst Michael Barone notes,
"In the 1970s, every southern state, including even West Virginia, grew faster than the national average, as did every state in
the West. No Midwestern states and no states in the Northeast,
except three small New England states, did so."[1] All this added
up to, as one urban historian has put it, an Age of Urban Crisis.[2] New York City, Philadelphia, Cleveland, Detroit, and Cin-

cinnati either defaulted on their financial obligations or came perilously close to fiscal collapse. Not only did wholesale urban renewal fail to revive cities, it seemed to have had exactly the opposite effect.

The planner Alexander Garvin, author of *The American City*, a comprehensive overview of city planning in the postwar period, begins his book with the following disclaimer: "One thing most people share . . . is disillusionment with urban planning as a way of fixing the American city."[3] While he stoutly argues that this disillusionment is not justified, he admits that "despite many remarkable successes, American city planning has been plagued with continuing mistakes."[4] Garvin is not referring to the City Beautiful movement or to the Garden City suburbs, which both remained popular—and successful—until the 1930s, when the Depression, and later the Second World War, put a stop to all construction and planning projects. He is describing the period 1950–70. The list of planning "mistakes" is long and includes urban renewal that failed to revive faltering downtowns; wholesale slum clearance that displaced more people than it housed; high-rise public housing that ill served the poor; cultural, sports, and government "centers" that were isolated from the rest of the city; and urban expressways that severed and blighted entire neighborhoods. All in all, a dismal record.

That the failure was so consistent and so widespread was the result of several factors. The postwar euphoria of the 1950s put a high premium on the notion of "newness," and any new idea, no matter how raw and untested, seemed worth trying. Public housing, for example, changed radically. The public housing that had been built immediately after the Housing Act of

1937 was similar to the urban housing being built by the private sector—unassuming row houses, each with a front door and a private backyard. The assumption was that poor people wanted to live like everyone else. By the 1950s, well-meaning social reformers promoted a new type of Radiant City housing, in which high-rise apartments replaced houses, balconies replaced backyards, and open space replaced streets and sidewalks.

The problem, as Mumford caustically observed, was that the promised City in a Park usually turned out to be a City in a Parking Lot.[5] Municipal housing agencies lacked the funds to provide landscaping, proper maintenance, and adequate policing, and when federal laws were passed forbidding the screening of tenants, The Projects soon turned into socially dysfunctional concentrations of poverty. Lobbies and corridors were vandalized, elevators broke down, staircases became garbage dumps, roofs leaked, and broken windows remained unreplaced. Without babysitters, single mothers were stranded in their apartments, and teenagers roamed unsupervised sixteen floors below.[6] As repairs were indefinitely deferred, many of the dilapidated apartments became unoccupiable. After only two decades, desperate municipal housing agencies often gave up. The first major housing project to be demolished—in 1972—was Pruitt-Igoe, a large housing complex in Saint Louis.

The dynamiting of Pruitt-Igoe was an iconic moment since the project had won a design award for its architect, Minoru Yamasaki (who later designed the World Trade Center towers in New York), but the demolition was to be repeated scores of time. Over the next two decades, public housing units in Baltimore, Philadelphia, and Detroit suffered similar fates, as did the 4,321 units of Robert Taylor Homes in Chicago. That was the other aspect of the failure: it was widespread. The uniform education received by architects and planners ensured that similar ideas were promoted from city to city. Since American cities compete for residents as well as employers, they tend "to keep up with the Joneses." If Los Angeles got rid of its streetcars, then streetcars instantly became old-fashioned; if Chicago built an urban expressway, that became the model; if New York built a cultural center, smaller cities followed. Lincoln Center turned out as overblown and bombastic as Jacobs and others had predicted. Boston's new government center was an unpopular, windswept nine-acre plaza around City Hall and resisted all efforts to introduce human activity. Chicago's Civic Center (now Daley) Plaza fared somewhat better, although it never quite managed to achieve the status of a great public place.

Vertical living, cultural complexes, and large plazas were integral to Le Corbusier's urban ideal; so was separating cars from pedestrians. Traffic separation had been introduced to American downtowns by the Viennese-born architect and planner Victor Gruen in his 1956 plan for Fort Worth, Texas, which provided raised decks for pedestrians. Although the proposal was not implemented because of public opposition to its cost, it was widely admired by city planners, and many cities built weather-protected downtown pedestrian-only systems. Streets in the air, or skyways, were built in Minneapolis, Saint Paul, and Calgary, Alberta; underground concourses appeared in Dallas, Houston, Philadelphia, and Montreal. In cities with climatic extremes, the heated and air-conditioned spaces were popular, but it was unclear that the convenience of weather protection was worth the high cost. Advocates said yes, but critics pointed out that dividing pedestrians between indoor walkways and outdoor sidewalks only diluted activity in both areas and had an adverse effect on the vitality of city streets.[7]

A less expensive pedestrianization strategy was to close selected streets to traffic and add benches, landscaping, and fountains. There were three options: semi-malls, in which sidewalks were widened and traffic lanes narrowed (usually to two, without parking); transit malls, which had a single bus lane and were closed to other vehicles; and full-fledged pedestrian malls, which were closed to all traffic. In 1957, the first pedestrian mall was built in Kalamazoo, Michigan. Over the following two decades, more than two hundred North American cities undertook similar pedestrianization measures. The problem with malls, as Jane Jacobs wrote at the time, was that "planned pedestrian street schemes, *if* they throw formidable borders for moving and parked cars around inherently weak and fragmentary preserves, *can introduce more problems than they solve* [emphasis in original]."[8] In short, once the novelty wore off, people—that is, shoppers—found that they didn't like pedestrian malls, preferring traditional streets with sidewalks. Businesses along malls suffered, stores relocated, and the deserted pedestrian malls soon became magnets for vagrants. Only about thirty pedestrian malls remain in operation today. Most are in college towns, such as Boulder, Colorado, Charlottesville, Virginia, and Burlington, Vermont, where large populations of students, living in proximity to downtown, have free time to populate the mall's cafés and bars. Some tourist-oriented Sunbelt cities, such as Santa Monica, Miami Beach, and Las Vegas, also have successful pedestrian malls. But malls elsewhere remain moribund or have been done away with altogether. The Kalamazoo mall has been reopened to limited vehicular traffic; Main Street Mall in Poughkeepsie has become a street again, as has Chicago's State Street. A transit mall on Philadelphia's Chestnut Street also reopened to traffic, although only after the previously thriving shopping street had suffered a marked decline, another victim of the Radiant City.

During the postwar era, modernist architects and critics attacked the City Beautiful movement for its Frenchified neoclassical taste and its elite aesthetic aspirations and championed the "city practical" instead. Yet civic art made a comeback in an unexpected guise. The 1965 demolition of McKim, Mead & White's Pennsylvania Station in New York spurred the formation of the historic preservation movement, which was motivated as much by an admiration for beauty as by an interest in history. Not coincidentally, most of the cherished civic landmarks date from the same era, and in most cities historic preservation really means City Beautiful preservation. The great train stations, for example—Union Station in Washington, D.C., 30th Street Station in Philadelphia, Grand Central Station in New York, and Union Station in Los Angeles—have been restored to their former eminence.

Buildings such as Washington's Union Station remind us that the City Beautiful era represents the benchmark for successful urban architecture. In a 2007 national poll that asked people to name their favorite buildings in the United States, the leading choices include the Jefferson Memorial, the Lincoln Memorial, the Supreme Court of the United States,

the National Gallery of Art in Washington, D.C., the Philadelphia Museum of Art, and the Chicago Tribune Tower—
all built between 1925 and 1943. In the top fifty favorites are
the Empire State Building, the Woolworth Building, and the
Chrysler Building, as well as the St. Regis Hotel, the Waldorf-
Astoria Hotel, Grand Central Station, and the New York Public
Library—and that's just in New York City. In all, architecture
from the four decades between 1900 and 1940 comprises more
than half of the top fifty buildings on the list, a remarkable sta-
tistic given the amount of construction that has taken place
since 1940.[9]

How has Ebenezer Howard's Garden City idea fared? The
last garden suburbs were built in the decade preceding the
Great Depression, but they remain alive in the public con-
sciousness for one simple reason: almost all the garden suburbs that were built between 1900 and 1930, such as Forest
Hills Gardens and Palos Verdes Estates, have survived and
prospered.[10] Hence, contemporary home buyers do not associate garden suburbs with a musty planning theory but rather
with desirable real estate. In the 1980s, the planning ideas of
Raymond Unwin and John Nolen resurfaced as what came to
be called New Urbanism. New Urbanism started in the 1980s
with Seaside, not a garden suburb but a tiny resort village on
the Florida Panhandle. Seaside had an influence far beyond its
small size. American home buyers were attracted by the picturesque, traditional architecture; developers, who generally paid
little attention to design, took note of the financial success. The
chief lessons of New Urbanism were that home buyers value
planning and design and will accept higher densities when
these are associated with a sense of community.

Witold Rybczynski

The garden suburb returns as New Urbanism
in a planned community in Orlando, Florida.

The resulting new generation of planned communities, such as Kentlands in Maryland, Stapleton in Colorado, I'On in South Carolina, and Baldwin Park and Celebration in Florida, adapt the old garden suburb model to present realities of higher land prices, greater car ownership, and a more competitive housing market. The resulting communities lack some of the nuance of the originals—vinyl siding and snap-on shutters have replaced solid masonry and craftsmanship—and tend to be larger than their small-scale predecessors. Celebration will have twenty thousand residents, Stapleton, thirty thousand. However, the basic tenets established by Unwin remain: compactness and variety in design, heterogeneity in house types, walkability, and a compact appearance of neighborliness. Above all, there is his chief lesson that in planning new communities much can be learned from the past, from the "individuality of towns." The new generation of garden suburbs draws from early-twentieth-century models, as well as from Colonial examples such as Charleston and Savannah. Detractors deride these historical influences as "neotraditional" and "nostalgic," but a sense of continuity with the past is precisely what appeals to home buyers.

Le Corbusier's urban theories proved largely unsuccessful, but they were not a complete failure. Towers-in-a-park were a resounding flop as a model for social housing, but high-rise urban living has succeeded for a different clientele. Apartment living in American cities predates the Radiant City, although the influence is definitely Parisian—the first, late-nineteenth-century New York apartments, patterned on Parisian models, were called French flats.[11] By the 1920s, with buildings such as the Ritz Tower, at forty-one stories the first residential skyscraper in the city; the twenty-seven-story San Remo; and its Art Deco cousin the El Dorado, all designed by Emory Roth, apartment living in New York was in full swing.[12] Roth was a proponent of the so-called Italian skyscraper—the twin San Remo towers are capped by classical temples; the top of the Beresford, another Roth design, has three cupolas. The apartments in these striking buildings were large, with salons and drawing rooms, roof gardens and solariums, servants' rooms and butlers' pantries. Eighteen-room suites, as well as duplex, or two-story, apartments, were not uncommon. Thus roof terraces, two-story apartments, and "villas in the sky" were well established in New York City years before Le Corbusier proposed them in the Radiant City. Nevertheless, that the most desirable New York apartments look out over Central Park to some extent validates his vision of towers surrounded by greenery.* So does the recent fashion for living in all-glass, distinctly modernist apartment towers. The big difference is that this is luxury housing, with doormen and janitors, in-house services and domestics, opulent kitchens, and marble bathrooms—all bourgeois amenities that Le Corbusier would have detested.

Jane Jacobs's rediscovery of the pleasures of downtown living seems, at first glance, to have been a runaway success. At the time she died, in 2006, she was widely recognized as the most influential urban thinker of her time. *The Death and Life of Great American Cities* has become the dominant book about city planning of the second half of the twentieth century—perhaps of the entire century. Few people read Unwin or Nolen anymore, and while Mumford's essays have preserved their crackling intelligence, *The City in History* now seems ponderous and dated. Jacobs's book, on the other hand, has changed the way succeeding generations of architects and planners think about cities, and it had an effect on cities themselves. "Lively, diverse, intense cities contain the seeds of their own regeneration," she wrote, "with energy enough to carry over for problems and needs outside themselves."[13] The second half of her statement never quite came true. The suburbanization of America, which she chose largely to ignore, was too advanced and too popular. But the revivals of many American downtowns, the

---

*The same combination of luxury high-rise living and open space happens in other cities: in Philadelphia the most exclusive apartments overlook Rittenhouse Square, in Chicago they look out over Lake Michigan, in San Francisco they have views of the Bay.

industrial lofts converted into residences, the restored historic districts, and the downtown residential real estate booms in cities such as New York, Boston, Philadelphia, Chicago, and San Francisco are a testament to her vision.

Yet that vision is playing out differently than what she expected. Jacobs's description of the urban good life has wide appeal, but the supply of dense urban neighborhoods with the requisite mix of street life, old architecture, diversity—and employment—is limited. Not many cities have downtown residential neighborhoods with the character of Greenwich Village. Strong demand and a small supply has produced the inevitable result: real estate values in Jacobite neighborhoods have gone through the roof, and the lively working-class districts that she championed have turned into exclusive enclaves, closed to all but the wealthy. Jacobs believed that the everyday amenities of city life should be available to everyone; little did she imagine that they would become exclusive luxuries instead.

Or maybe she did imagine it. Despite that *Death and Life* has become a canonic planning text, the book is intensely suspicious of centralized planning and champions individual choice and free markets. A decade ago, Roger Montgomery, a noted city planner, pointed out that the arguments put forward in *Death and Life* reflect an active distrust of government, an endorsement of small business, and an almost total lack of attention to the role of corporations in American cities. He described the book as an "early neo-conservative tract," whose themes "look mighty like the core belief system of libertarian conservatism."[14] Jacobs a libertarian conservative? I asked Nathan Glazer, who was her editor in the 1960s, whether he agreed. "Certainly somewhat libertarian, definitely not conservative," he replied.

"In a sense, *anarchistic* would be a better term than *libertarian*—people making their own decisions, with less or no guidance or control from above, will make a better city."

Jacobs's "better city" is a curiously classless place. *Death and Life* had little to say about social and economic differences, and even less about race, and reflected the author's values as a middle-class, young woman from an industrial city living in a working-class neighborhood, and in love with the hustle and bustle of New York.[15] Perhaps that is why she appeared perplexed by the massive movement to the suburbs that was taking place even as she was writing her book. The perceptions that some people might prefer suburban quiet to urban bustle, and that Greenwich Village might not appeal to everyone, eluded her.

They did not elude Herbert J. Gans, a sociologist who had guided Jacobs around Boston's North End when she was writing her book. In a 1962 review of *Death and Life*, Gans pointed out that neighborhoods such as Greenwich Village and Chicago's Back-of-the-Yards, which are described as models of urbanism in *Death and Life*, are actually highly unusual. Gans, who studied Boston's West End closely for his own book *The Urban Villagers*, argued that such downtown, working-class, ethnic enclaves, with their collections of small stores and quaint buildings, were very different not only from middle-class neighborhoods but also from most other urban working-class neighborhoods. Moreover, they were anachronisms, with small houses, no private gardens, and no space for parking and "built for a style of life which is going out of fashion with the large majority of Americans who are free to choose their place of residence," he wrote.[16] Gans also observed that vitality and liveliness were not necessarily universally desired. He'd found no evidence that middle-class people, who were the majority of the urban population, valued such attributes. "They do not want the visible vitality of a North End," he pointed out, "but rather the quiet and the privacy obtainable in low-density neighborhoods and elevator apartment houses."[17]

The revitalization of some downtowns has not proved Gans wrong. The downtown neighborhoods that have become popular have also been transformed—"gentrified"—into upper-middle-class places that bear little resemblance to Jacobs's Greenwich Village. "Visible vitality" has proved attractive, but chiefly to young professionals, childless couples, and retirees, and except in New York City, the suburbs remain the preferred location for families with children.

Gans, who had taught in a city-planning department, took issue with Jacobs's critique of city planning. Not because he was particularly sympathetic to planners—although he pointed out that most city planners probably agreed with her proposals—but because he felt that she exaggerated the power of planning in American society. "The truth is that the new forms of residential building—in suburb as well as city—are not products of orthodox planning theory," he wrote, "but expressions of middle-class culture which guides the housing market, and which planners also serve."[18] In an entrepreneurial society where people are free to choose how, and where, to live, they will ultimately get what they want, not what planners think they need.

Gans's insight underlines that while planners and architects propose concepts such as the City Beautiful or garden suburbs, the public ultimately decides what it likes and dislikes. Instead of one big idea, the city is formed by many little ideas, "the freedom of countless numbers of people to make and carry out countless plans," as Jacobs put it.[19] The results can be unexpected, and often not what planners anticipated. While City Beautiful advocates wanted to beautify the entire city, the public liked downtown monumental buildings. Le Corbusier saw towers in the park as worker housing, but high-rise living turned out to be most popular among the wealthy. Wright imagined Broadacre City as a place for independent yeomen farmers, but decentralized development attracts independent software developers, and Walmart, instead. The New Urbanism movement has grand ambitions to remake the center of cities, but its greatest successes have been in the suburbs, so much so that Vincent Scully, an admirer, once wrote, "The New Suburbanism might be a truer label."[20]

In 1968, the eminent city planner Martin Meyerson described the challenges facing American cities: "The greatest need in our cities is not so much for a giant rebuilding program as for a giant upsurge of popular concern for and pride in the urban environment."[21] Meyerson meant that in a representative democracy the expenditure of public funds on urban renewal, public housing, and highway construction requires a political constituency. Forty years later, that constituency expresses itself in the form of individual choices, and individual demands, channeled through the marketplace. Or, as my old schoolmate Andrejs Skaburskis, a city planner at Queen's University in Canada, pithily put it, echoing Gans, "In the long run, it is the demand-side pressures that forge the shape of cities."[22] That might just be the next big planning idea: the public actually knows what it wants or, at least, recognizes it when it sees it.

6

* ▪ ■ ▪ *

Arcades and Malls, Big Boxes
and Lifestyle Centers

If the first half of the twentieth century in American urbanism—the era of the City Beautiful movement, the garden suburbs, and urban renewal—can be characterized as the Age of
Planning, the period after 1970 was the Age of the Market. To
understand the implications of an urbanism based on popular demand, it helps to look at an environment where the consumer is paramount: the places where we shop. Shopping
habits have changed radically over time. A century ago, shoppers dressed up and took a streetcar to a downtown department
store; fifty years ago they drove the station wagon to a suburban shopping center; and twenty-five years ago they might have
spent the afternoon at the mall. Today, many young people
have never seen a true department store (most so-called department stores sell chiefly apparel and cosmetics), and I suspect
that in another twenty-five years many shoppers will never have
set foot in a mall.

Although many of the changes to shopping places have had a significant impact on the physical shape of the city, they have generally originated with merchants and businessmen, rather than with city planners and architects. The origins of the American shopping mall, for example, can be found in the decision of an eighteenth-century Parisian entrepreneur, a certain M. Langlois, to buy a narrow alley and the adjoining properties behind the Théâtre Feydeau in the second arrondissement and, by the simple expedient of adding a glass roof, to turn a squalid lane into a protected shopping street. The size of the so-called Passage Feydeau (which opened in 1791 and was demolished in 1824) can be judged by the number of its tenants: several milliners and haberdashers, two book stalls, a florist, a tobacconist, a stamp dealer, a chestnut seller, and, along the entire length of the upper floor, an *estaminet* (a distinctly unfancy type of café that permitted smoking).[1]

Since Parisian streets were dirty and ill-maintained (this was before Haussmann's fine boulevards), these weather-protected pedestrian ways, open at each end and serving as convenient shortcuts, became extremely popular. By 1840 the city had more than a hundred *passages*, many with exotic names such as Prado, Caire, and Panoramas. Their glass and cast-iron roofs, which would later become common in conservatories, exhibition halls, and railroad stations, were a novelty; so was gas lighting, whose first use in a public space occurred in a Parisian *passage*.

The London version of the *passage* was the arcade. The first was the Royal Opera Arcade, which was built in 1816–18 next to the Haymarket Opera (since burned). It was designed by the famous architect John Nash, who covered the long, narrow

Burlington Arcade in London, an early example
of urban design created by entrepreneurship.

space with a series of vaults topped by glass domes and fitted
the shop-fronts with delicate bow windows. Regency arcades
were grander than their Parisian counterparts. The Burlington Arcade in Piccadilly, for example, housed seventy-two
two-story shops and sported liveried attendants. The beautiful Royal Arcade, built in 1879, was so named because it was
where Queen Victoria had her riding skirts made. Joseph Pax-
ton, who built the Crystal Palace, proposed an enormous glass-
roofed arcade more than a hundred feet high and ten miles
long. That ambitious project was never realized, but monumental glass-roofed arcades appeared in Brussels, Berlin,
Naples, Saint Petersburg, and Moscow. The most impressive
was in Milan, the Galleria Vittorio Emanuele II, a beautiful
structure with four glass-vaulted arms meeting in a hexagonal

dome. Several glass-roofed arcades were built in North America: a Greek Revival arcade in Providence, Rhode Island, that opened as early as 1829; a block-long arcade in Toronto; an impressive five-story structure in Cleveland; and the Gothic Revival Arcade Building in downtown Saint Louis.

The Saint Louis arcade, which opened in 1919, was late on the scene, for by then fashionable downtown shoppers were drawn to a new venue: the department store. Only ten years after the first department store opened in Paris in 1838, the New York City merchant Alexander Turney Stewart built the Marble Palace, a grand multistory building that resembled a Renaissance palazzo, across the street from City Hall, and twenty-four years later expanded into an eight-story building featuring an open central space covered by a ninety-foot-tall glass dome. Like the London arcades, department stores were intended to convey an atmosphere of luxury and glamour—and technological progress: they were the first public buildings to have electric lighting and passenger elevators. Department store owners frequently turned to prominent architects. In 1885–87, for example, Chicago's Marshall Field brought H. H. Richardson from Boston to build a seven-story Romanesque-style store that occupied half a city block. A decade later, two German-born Chicago merchants, Leopold Schlesinger and David Mayer, commissioned Dankmar Adler and Louis Sullivan to build their main store on the corner of State and Madison. For his flagship store, the pioneering Philadelphia merchandiser John Wanamaker hired Daniel Burnham, who was then designing Union Station. Burnham produced a spectacular five-story central atrium that reverberated to the sounds of the world's largest pipe organ.

Department stores not only sold a variety of goods under

one roof, but the merchandise was openly displayed and—
another novelty—had price tags. Department stores sold everything—apparel, furniture, toys, appliances, and hardware—and
included food departments and beauty salons, as well as tea-
rooms and restaurants. Extravagant window displays were a
holiday tradition; so was a visit to the store's Santa Claus. In a
period without national chains and national advertising, shoppers recognized and trusted the downtown department stores—
Macy's in New York, Filene's in Boston, Hudson's in Detroit,
the Emporium in San Francisco, Eaton's in Montreal.

Department stores dominated downtown retailing for a hundred years, and when families started to move to the suburbs in
the postwar period, the department stores moved with them. As
early as 1930, the downtown Philadelphia merchandizer Straw-
bridge & Clothier built a branch in Ardmore on the Main Line.
Named Suburban Square, the cluster of Art Deco buildings
comprised a multifloor department store surrounded by smaller
shops around an outdoor concourse—an early shopping center. In the late 1940s, similar developments appeared in Los
Angeles, Beverly, Massachusetts, and Columbus, Ohio, but the
lasting model for the full-fledged regional shopping center was
Seattle's Northgate. The complex was built north of the city
by the owner of Bon Marché, a downtown department store.
Opened in 1950, the center consisted of a three-story department store and seventeen shops, including a supermarket and
a bank (a movie theater and a bowling alley were added a few
years later). The architect of the center, John Graham Jr., lined
up the stores on two sides of an open-air promenade and surrounded the building by a parking lot for four thousand cars.
The landscaped promenade was pleasant for pedestrians, and

the parking lot was convenient for drivers, although the inside-out arrangement produced a bland exterior of blank walls and truck bays.

Shopping center builders followed a simple formula: identify a location adjacent to a highway interchange; provide plenty of free parking; and use a department store to "anchor" the center and attract smaller tenants. The formula worked. By 1960 the United States had four thousand shopping centers. Northgate included a single department store, but the standard arrangement, called a dumbbell plan, had two department stores, one at each end of a pedestrian promenade. Sometimes the promenade included an open gallery and stores on a second level. A significant design innovation occurred in 1956 in Edina, Minnesota, a suburb of Minneapolis, when the Dayton Company, which owned a downtown department store, built the first fully enclosed mall. The architect Victor Gruen, originally a Viennese, said that he was inspired by Milan's Galleria, although the Southdale arcade was entirely enclosed rather than open at the ends.[2] Heated and air-conditioned shopping malls were expensive to build and operate, but they proved extremely popular and quickly became the industry standard. To attract more shoppers, the malls added not only movie theaters and restaurants, but also banks, health clubs, medical centers, and even noncommercial services such as post offices and libraries. The form of the shopping mall may have been inspired by urban arcades, but malls became, in effect, the self-sufficient roadside markets that Frank Lloyd Wright had imagined two decades earlier. The largest malls included several anchor stores and exceeded 1 million square feet; so-called megamalls, such as the West Edmonton Mall in Alberta, Canada, and the Mall of America outside Minneapolis, could be as large as 6 million square feet, housing amusement parks and hotels as well as stores.

Suburban shopping malls were so successful during the 1970s and 1980s that many cities, still struggling to revitalize their downtowns and smarting from the failures of urban renewal, turned to mall developers for help. Despite their roots in urban *passages* and arcades, shopping malls seemed ill suited to downtown. Suburban malls were built on cheap land, but urban land was expensive, which constrained design in two important ways. As developers of suburban malls discovered, shoppers will climb only one flight of stairs; hence suburban malls typically have two floors. The small sites of urban malls required four to six floors, and urban developers had a difficult time attracting merchants to the upper levels.*[3] Expensive land imposed a second constraint: with insufficient space for surface parking, multistory parking structures were required. But a parking garage costs ten times as much to build as a simple lot.[4] Municipalities attempted to overcome this obstacle by building and operating the parking structures themselves. Such concessions, as well as other financial incentives, encouraged developers to build large downtown shopping malls in a number of cities.[5]

Shopping malls in the suburbs thrived because shoppers could easily drive to malls and park nearby. Urban shopping

---

*The old department stores regularly had six floors, but the upper levels were reserved for less frequented departments, such as those selling furniture and appliances. The most popular items, such as clothing, were always on the lower levels; toy departments were generally halfway up.

malls cannot provide the same convenience: drivers have to navigate congested city streets, and parking garages are neither convenient nor free. Moreover, suburban malls are self-contained—there isn't anywhere else to go—whereas urban malls are surrounded by scores of competing stores, restaurants, and other attractions. As a result, the financial record of urban shopping malls has been checkered. Researchers Bernard Frieden and Lynne Sagalyn suggest that while urban malls may be profitable for lenders (who incorporate high-risk premiums) and merchants (since sales per square foot in urban malls are generally high, at least on the lower levels), they are not always profitable for developers, since the up-front and operating costs are much higher than in the suburbs.[6] Nor have urban malls had the hoped-for effect of rejuvenating downtowns. Instead, the marketing strategy of grouping national name-brand stores in clean, hospitable environments has drained pedestrian and commercial life from nearby streets. The Gallery at Market East, a multilevel mall in downtown Philadelphia, for example, is full of shoppers, but adjacent Market Street, once the city's chief shopping street, now attracts only discount merchants and dollar stores.

In the late 1990s, suburban shopping malls, too, began to falter. Overbuilding produced too many malls, and architectural complexity and luxurious materials drove construction costs to levels that exceeded potential rental income. Shopping habits were also changing. With two-income families becoming the norm, people were more interested in convenience and efficiency than in spending hours walking around a huge shopping mall. Moreover, the traditional department store, which was the mainstay of the shopping center concept, was in trouble. Specialty retailers were undercutting many of the department stores' prices so that department stores were no longer the cheapest places to buy brand-name running shoes, toys, furniture, bath towels—or almost anything.

Shoppers now had a new alternative: the big-box store.* The big-box format emerged in the mid-1980s. The merchandising concept is simple: sell the same goods as traditional retailers, but at notably lower prices. According to economists Peter Linneman and Deborah Moy, between 1993 and 2003 "at least ninety percent of the growth in retail sales has gone to big-box retailers."[7] Many of these boxes belong to Walmart, the corporation that has revolutionized shopping in America (and increasingly around the globe).† Walmart has mastered the art of delivering goods directly from the manufacturer to the consumer, and it does so for a bewildering variety of products: T-shirts, toys, tires, T-bone steaks, and tiaras, as well as banking services, medical prescriptions, and insurance. The average store exceeds one hundred thousand square feet and some can be more than twice that size.

The other retailers who successfully adopted the big-box format are discount clubs, which resemble Walmart but charge a membership fee; factory outlets, which sell discontinued or discounted goods; and specialty retailers, who carry a single product type such as home-improvement materials, knocked-down furniture, electronic equipment, or clothing. What all these big boxes have in common, in addition to size

---

*Also called superstores or megastores; in Europe they are sometimes referred to as hypermarkets.

†Walmart arrived in China in 1996 and over the next decade opened sixty-nine stores there.

A ubiquitous big-box store in Shenzhen, China.

and lower prices, is self-service. The consumer pushes her shopping cart up and down the aisles alongside a large variety of goods undramatically displayed on utilitarian shelves and racks, collects the merchandise, and exits via a checkout counter. The focus is on increasing convenience while reducing overhead and providing the consumer with an extremely wide range of choices at low prices.

The ancestor of the big box was a grocery store that opened in 1916 in Memphis, the brainchild of local merchant Clarence Saunders. Customers in Saunders's grocery entered through a turnstile at one end of the store, picked up wire baskets, and, following a predetermined route between rows of shelves, exited through a checkout counter at the other end. This was shopping reconceived as an assembly line. There were only two clerks, one at the cash register and one to restock the shelves. Saunders

patented his idea and created a successful franchise called Piggly Wiggly, which eventually expanded to no less than twenty-six
hundred outlets across the South and Midwest.[8] Piggly Wiggly
stores were relatively small, but self-service grocers soon grew
in size, adding parking lots and becoming what people called
supermarkets.

The device that enabled the supermarket to develop into
a big box was the humble shopping cart. In 1936, Sylvan N.
Goldman, an Oklahoma supermarket-chain owner, introduced
a wheeled frame that was capable of carrying two removable
baskets; when not in use, the frame collapsed to save space. It
took another decade for the shopping cart to assume its present
form: a large wheeled basket, with a rear flap that allows carts to
be nested inside one another for compact storage. Ungainly and
crude, the lowly shopping cart has remained unaltered for seventy years, making up in practicality what it lacks in elegance.

Big-box stores proved so successful that they spawned a new
kind of suburban shopping place, the power center. A power
center consists of several big boxes (as few as three, as many as a
dozen) arranged around a large parking lot. Unlike a shopping
mall, a power center has no small shops, the entrances to the big
boxes are far apart, and if you have to go to more than one store,
you drive. There are no enclosed common areas—shoppers are
not directed, or even encouraged, to visit more than one store; if
you want a flat-screen television, you drive to one box; if it's toilet
paper you're after, you drive to another. The economic rationale
for a power center is nearby highway access and a shared parking
lot; sociability, that staple of traditional shopping places—even
malls—is entirely absent.

Big-box stores appeared first in suburban locations, but as

retailers sought new markets, the concept migrated to the city. The big-box store has adapted to urban conditions more successfully than the shopping mall, although urban big boxes tend to be smaller than their suburban counterparts (apartment dwellers have less storage space, so they tend not to buy in bulk). Urban big boxes are often organized on several floors and, at least in Manhattan, dispense with parking lots. They also usually lack delivery bays for large trailer trucks, since deliveries are made by smaller vehicles that bring goods from intermediate distribution centers at the edge of the city. Despite such logistical challenges, urban density makes big-box stores extremely profitable. In 2008, Home Depot opened its *third* Manhattan store, in the Bloomberg Tower on Fifty-ninth Street and Third Avenue; Costco, the largest membership warehouse-club chain in the world, has built a 147,000-square-foot store in a new residential development in downtown Vancouver, British Columbia; and IKEA, the Swedish furniture retailer, has opened a 346,000-square-foot store in the Red Hook neighborhood of Brooklyn.

I always feel a little depressed when I visit a big-box store. The experience is a considerable step down from even a shopping mall, whose interior at least has natural light, fountains, and trees. Shopping mall developers did not set their architectural sights high compared to the builders of the elegant arcades and palatial department stores, but the design of a big-box store is governed entirely by economy. Basically, a one-story warehouse is built in the least expensive manner: plain exteriors, painted steel columns, utilitarian lighting, no attempt at decoration.

The impression given to the shopper, confirmed by the low prices, is that everything possible is done to keep overhead to a minimum and to pass the savings on to the consumer. This is the opposite of the department store's shopping-as-glamour, or the mall's shopping-as-fun; this is shopping-as-utility.

Although the big-box store signals the triumph of a lifestyle that values convenience, price, and anonymity, it does not signal the end of leisurely shopping. Shoppers don't just want fast-and-convenient, they also want slow-and-relaxed. The setting for the latter can be a traditional main street, a farmers' market, or a so-called lifestyle center.[9] Lifestyle centers, which are built and managed by a single owner and contain the same sorts of national chain stores as malls, are distinguished chiefly by their design. Basically outdoor shopping malls—sometimes referred to as topless malls—these have streets and sidewalks rather than indoor pedestrian arcades. The storefronts face the street, restaurants spill out onto broad sidewalks, and small parks and squares further enliven the streetscape; cars are parked on the street, in garages, and in discreetly hidden lots. While 1990s shopping mall developers built amenities such as amusement parks, the lifestyle center revives traditional urban experiences such as outdoor dining, strolling, and people-watching.

Lifestyle centers do more than mix people and cars, however; they add other uses.* Victory Park, for example, a lifestyle center on the northern fringe of downtown Dallas, includes four thousand residential units, as well as office space, a thirty-three-

---

*Mixed-use lifestyle centers should not be confused with themed shopping places such as Universal CityWalk in Los Angeles, Downtown Disney in Anaheim, or La Encantada in Tucson, which have outdoor public spaces but contain only retail uses.

story hotel, and a professional-basketball arena.[10] Although the architecture of the early lifestyle centers, such as Mizner Park in Boca Raton, and Santana Row in San Jose, is distinctly old-fashioned and intended to recall a small-town Main Street of the early twentieth century, more recent projects have adopted edgier architectural styles, with expanses of glass, modern materials, and industrial-looking details.[11]

Since lifestyle centers use land intensively, do not have heated and air-conditioned public spaces, and usually dispense with anchor tenants (who in a mall pay little or no rent), they are cheaper to operate than traditional malls. However, financing, designing, and building a high-density, mixed-use lifestyle center is more complicated than building a single-use shopping mall. Achieving a lively mix of retail, residential, and commercial also requires a relatively affluent population that can afford the upscale shops and high-end residential units. The important question for developers is whether lifestyle centers will have the same drawing power as the traditional anchor department stores, and whether shoppers will accept the open-air format after having enjoyed several decades of air-conditioned and heated malls. So far, the answer seems to be a qualified yes—as long as the town center is located in a prosperous, growing region and in a mild climate.

While some lifestyle centers are in isolated locations, they work best when they are part of an existing city. CityPlace, in downtown West Palm Beach, for example, has played a central role in reviving this previously moribund downtown. Apartments and condominiums are combined with six hundred thousand square feet of retail space, more than twenty restaurants and clubs, a twenty-screen cinema, and an old church that has been converted into a cultural center. In Rockville, Maryland, a suburb of Washington, D.C., a fifteen-acre section of downtown that included an abandoned shopping mall (built as part of a 1970s urban-renewal project) and a strip mall has been converted into a lifestyle center called Rockville Town Square. The uses include retail space at street level, more than six hundred apartments on upper floors, a public library, a community center, and parking garages. The center covers several city blocks and includes a town square. The project is a joint venture of the city, the county (which built the library), a retail developer, and a residential developer.[12] The presence of a library and a community center signals a growing trend in lifestyle centers: incorporating nonretail uses such as theaters and schools.

When mixed-use centers grow large enough, and dense enough, they function almost like big-city downtowns. The model for the planned downtown is Reston Town Center in Virginia, twenty miles from Washington, D.C. Reston, a pioneering planned community on 6,750 acres of Fairfax County farmland, was founded in the 1960s by developer Robert E. Simon (hence RESton). His concept, loosely based on the Garden City model, was an alternative to sprawling postwar suburbs: the projected population of sixty thousand was housed in five clustered residential neighborhoods, called villages, surrounded by woods and unbuilt countryside. In addition to small neighborhood centers, Simon also planned to build a high-density town center.

The first neighborhood center, Lake Anne Village, opened in 1965 and garnered national attention for its modernist architecture (designed by architects Julian H. Whittlesey, William J. Conklin, and Cloethiel Woodward Smith) and its picturesque lakeside plan, said to be influenced by the Italian seaside town of Portofino.[13] However, for the main town center, Whittlesey and Conklin designed a conventional sixties megastructure, with all the functions in what was effectively a single building. Simon objected that this solution was too expensive, and too difficult to implement in phases, and suggested a more traditional approach using streets and sidewalks.[14] Instead, the planners, some of whom had been involved in the design of Radburn, proposed an all-pedestrian scheme, with car traffic and parking on a lower level. Before this could be built, the Gulf Oil Corporation, which was a major investor, bought out Simon and took control of the project. A planning firm from Philadelphia was commissioned to produce a third plan, which likewise separated pedestrians from cars, this time drawing inspiration from regional shopping malls and incorporating a glass-covered arcade. That wasn't built, either.

In 1978, Reston was taken over by a subsidiary of the Mobil Oil Corporation, and RTKL, a large Baltimore-based architecture and planning firm, was hired to take yet another stab at the town center. This time, influenced by *The Death and Life of Great American Cities* and the failures of large-scale urban projects, the planners adopted a less radical approach. Instead of creating superblocks and pedestrian malls, they laid out a more or less conventional grid of streets and sidewalks, with relatively small blocks subdivided into building lots. This plan allowed construction on the five hundred acres to unfold gradually, and more naturally, over the next three decades. The character of the project also changed, from a high-density suburban center to a full-fledged business district, with an emphasis on office space. Largely complete today, Reston Town Center aims for a daytime

People, sidewalks, and cars in a planned
downtown in Reston, Virginia.

population of eighty thousand people—office workers, shoppers, residents—and a residential population of six thousand.[15] That makes a net residential density of seventy-five people per acre, lower than in Manhattan, but exceeding that of most American downtowns.

The business model for Reston Town Center was influenced by nearby Tysons Corner. Tysons Corner is an early and large example of a phenomenon that Joel Garreau christened "edge city."[16] An edge city is a suburban concentration of offices, shops, apartment buildings, and entertainment venues distinguished by its large scale (Tysons Corner is the nation's twelfth-largest business district and draws fifty-five thousand shoppers a day), and its urban density (Tysons Corner is denser than downtown Miami). "[Edge cities] look not at all like our old downtowns," observed Garreau. "Buildings rarely rise shoulder to shoulder, as in Chicago's Loop. Instead, their broad, low outlines dot the landscape like mushrooms, separated by greensward and parking lots."[17] The confusing mixture of office blocks, shopping malls, apartment buildings, and parking structures at Tysons Corner defies traditional urban categorization.

Reston Town Center, on the other hand, is immediately recognizable as a "downtown." Robert A. M. Stern, who designed one of the apartment complexes at Reston, has compared it to earlier suburban planned downtowns such as White Plains, New York; Stamford, Connecticut; and Evanston, Illinois.[18] Reston has twenty-story office towers and tall apartment buildings, a large hotel, and a cinema, as well as a central square with an open structure that in winter houses a skating rink (shades of Rockefeller Center). The buildings along the main street—Market Street—contain shops and restaurants at street level. Unlike many lifestyle centers, Reston Town Center is not architecturally themed; building styles vary from steel-and-glass contemporary to what Stern calls "moderne-inspired"—limestone and brick with setbacks and terraces.

This town center is a novel effort to apply the lessons of Jane Jacobs and traditional downtowns to a commercial real estate development. It mostly works. The sidewalks and public spaces are lively, and the streets and the assortment of high-rise buildings and storefronts don't feel "planned." Parking is handled in large aboveground garages that line the two sides of downtown. Perhaps one day these structures will be replaced by office buildings or apartment blocks with underground parking, but for the moment the row of parking structures form a somewhat dreary "back" to Market Street's lively "front."

The presence of so much parking is a reminder that this

downtown is, like a shopping mall, a place to which people drive.* Once they get there, they find the usual assortment of national chains, from Victoria's Secret to Starbucks; supermarkets, groceries, and hardware stores are located in an open-air shopping center nearby. As in a shopping mall, there are many eateries—no fewer than thirty. During a visit, I chose Clyde's of Reston for lunch. Despite its name, this restaurant is part of a local chain with outlets in Washington, D.C., and in suburban Maryland and northern Virginia. But the burger was good, and I enjoyed sitting outside on a warm spring day. My view from the terrace was of a small square with a fountain, park benches and street trees, women with strollers, children on scooters, pinstriped businessmen. The setting was familiar: cars parked on the street, wide sidewalks, storefronts, and shop windows. I was also struck by what I didn't see. No superblocks, no freestanding towers surrounded by parks, no windswept plazas, no vertical separation of cars and pedestrians, no indoor shopping malls. It was as if the urban renewal of the 1960s had never happened.

*An extension of the Washington, D.C., Metro is scheduled to reach Reston Town Center by 2015.

7

＊　▪　■　▪　＊

On the Waterfront

Active waterfronts are as much a hallmark of American cities today as busy sidewalks and skyscrapers were in the past. Not since waterfronts served as commercial ports and transportation hubs have they figured so prominently in city planning. When the citizens of Brooklyn Heights called for converting the disused piers along the East River into a park, they were following a pattern repeated in countless cities. Waterfronts today, whether along a deepwater harbor, a lake, or a river, represent some of the most desirable urban real estate—not only for parks, but also for museums, tourist attractions, recreational facilities, and commercial and residential developments. Reclaimed harbors (Boston, Baltimore, and Toronto), converted piers (New York and Philadelphia), restored waterfronts (Louisville and Seattle), and rehabilitated canals (Georgetown and Montreal) loom large as urban attractions. Even cities without old waterfronts are jumping on the bandwagon. Dallas, for example, recently launched an ambitious flood-control plan that will transform the area on the banks of the Trinity River into the nation's largest urban park.

Waterfronts are almost entirely absent in the big ideas of twentieth-century city planning. Camillo Sitte's *The Art of Building Cities*, for example, which had a powerful influence on Garden City planners, ignores waterfronts altogether. In his magisterial *Town Planning in Practice*, Raymond Unwin discusses the plan of medieval Nuremberg, but does not consider the Pegnitz River, which runs through the center of the old city, worth mentioning. Le Corbusier's "Contemporary City of Three Million Inhabitants" includes an industrial zone serviced by a barge canal that connects to a river that he purposely located some distance from the city center. "The river is a kind of liquid railway, a goods station and a sorting house," he observes. "In a decent house the servants' stairs do not go through the drawing-room—even if the maid is charming (or if the little boats delight the loiterer leaning on a bridge)."[1] In Frank Lloyd Wright's Broadacre City, the river passes indiscriminately through an industrial district, behind a roadside market, through a recreation area, next to the county seat, and then beside the sports arena parking lot.

Only the City Beautiful planners appreciated—and exploited—the potential of urban waterfronts. A characteristic early example is the Pennsylvania state capital of Harrisburg, which sits beside the Susquehanna River. In 1900, Harrisburg was a small city of only fifty thousand, sandwiched between a flood-prone creek and a muddy riverbank that functioned chiefly as a trash dump. The city fathers, encouraged by the impending construction of a new capitol building, launched an ambitious beautification campaign, which, according to historian William H. Wilson, was the first in the nation to use the phrase *City Beautiful* as a public rallying cry.[2] The extensive civic improvements, which included river dredging and flood control measures, as well as major sewers, street paving, and parks, took a decade and a half to implement. The Boston-based landscape architect, Warren H. Manning, was commissioned to prepare the master plan. Manning had spent eight years with Frederick Law Olmsted, where he had worked on park systems in Buffalo and Rochester, and would go on to design city and campus plans, public parks, garden suburbs, and private gardens, becoming, as one landscape historian writes, "one of the period's most prolific practitioners."[3]

Manning considered Harrisburg one of the most important projects of his fruitful career.[4] The master plan encompassed the whole city and included parkways, a 140-acre park centered on a lake created out of swampland, and the crowning jewel, a three-mile-long riverfront park. A winding drive and linear park along a curving bluff overlooked the river, while below a concrete promenade stabilized the bank at the water's edge. The park was linked by a pedestrian bridge to a large island in the middle of the river, where Manning planned athletic fields, a grandstand, and swimming facilities.

The design of the Harrisburg parks tends to the naturalistic, for although Manning played an instrumental role in founding the American Civic Association and the American Society of Landscape Architects, both bulwarks of the City Beautiful movement, he was not sympathetic to Beaux Arts–style planning and much preferred the picturesque approach of his mentor, Olmsted. "A splendid strip of green," runs a contemporary description of Riverfront Park, "giving a superb view over the unsurpassed panorama of river, island and mountains to the west and affording easily reached breathing spaces for a vast multitude of people."[5]

"Vast multitude" proved to be right; by 1912, the park system was attracting an estimated 1.6 million visits per year.[6] The island park today continues to be an active place, with playing fields, picnicking grounds, nature trails, marinas, a baseball stadium, and on the island's tip, a public beach. Riverfront Park remains an urban breathing space, just as Manning intended. On the warm summer day I visited, I saw walkers and joggers on the pathways, people eating their lunch at picnic tables, and fishermen on the promenade steps, dangling their lines in the Susquehanna.

The most ambitious urban waterfront proposal for a major American city was contained in Burnham and Bennett's 1909 *Plan of Chicago*. This document was commissioned by a group of progressive businessmen who were inspired by the work that Burnham, McKim, and Olmsted Jr. were doing on the McMillan Plan in Washington, D.C., and hoped to influence the development of their own city. The plan described Lake Michigan as one of Chicago's great natural assets and proposed lining the lakefront with a series of parks and a giant harbor for freight and passenger vessels as well as pleasure yachts. The south branch of the Chicago River would carry barge traffic, but with plenty of places for "delightful loitering" since the banks were modeled on Parisian quais, with streets overlooking lower-level wharfs. "The opportunity should be seized to plan a comprehensive and adequate development of the river banks," Burnham and Bennett wrote, "so that the commercial facilities shall be extended, while at the same time the aesthetic side of the problem shall be worked out."[7]

Burnham's *Plan of Chicago* made the river
an integral part of the city.

Although Burnham and Bennett's plan for Chicago was
not implemented, the idea of a lakefront park took hold. The
grounds of the World's Columbian Exposition were transformed into Jackson Park, and the lakefront opposite the Loop
was made into Grant Park, with sites for museums and other cultural buildings. Chicago was the only major American city with
a civic waterfront, for by the 1920s most cities had ignored the
"aesthetic side of the problem" for so long that rivers and lake-
fronts really did resemble the "liquid railways" of Le Corbusier's memorable characterization. Through the mid-twentieth
century, city waterfronts were so vital to the national economy
that most cities hadn't paused to consider any aesthetic func-

tion. Loading and unloading cargo was labor-intensive—and irregular, for ships arrived at indeterminate intervals—so ports depended on large workforces, permanently on call, which only cities could provide. Ports required not only stevedores and piers but also storage facilities and warehouses, as well as ships' chandlers, brokers, shippers, and various other intermediaries. The steamship-driven expansion of transoceanic travel with its tens of thousands of passengers added hotels, boardinghouses, and restaurants. Indeed, so great was the cumulative impact of all this maritime-related activity that, at least in North America, it was impossible to have a thriving urban economy without a port.* A protected harbor immediately accessible from the sea was best: Boston, New York, and Charleston on the Atlantic; Mobile, Houston, and New Orleans on the Gulf of Mexico; Vancouver, Seattle, San Francisco, Los Angeles, and San Diego on the Pacific. A deepwater port on a navigable river or bay—Montreal, Philadelphia, Baltimore, and Portland, Oregon—was almost as good. Cities were also built on major rivers and lakes: Cincinnati and Louisville prospered on the Ohio, as did Minneapolis, Saint Louis, and Memphis on the Mississippi, and Omaha and Kansas City on the Missouri; Toronto, Buffalo, Cleveland, Detroit, Milwaukee, and Chicago depended on the Great Lakes.

The advent of truck transportation and air travel altered the competitive advantage of cities with good harbors, since factories and warehouses were now located adjacent to highway interchanges and airports rather than near urban piers. But

---

*For historical reasons, Europe has many inland cities, such as Paris, Madrid, and Berlin, but all major American cities founded before the nineteenth century had an important commercial waterfront.

the chief agent of change for waterfront cities was the shipping
container. The first full-fledged example of container shipping occurred in April 1956, when a refitted Second World
War tanker, the *Ideal-X*, sailed from Newark carrying fifty-eight
containers—actually aluminum truck bodies with the wheels
removed. Arriving in Houston, the bodies were unloaded,
dropped onto trailer chassis, and hauled to their final destina-
tions. It signaled the beginning of a revolution in global transportation, for at a time when it cost $5.83 per ton to load loose
cargo onto a medium-size ship, the cost of loading a ton onto
the *Ideal-X* was just 15.8 cents.[8]

Containers are filled at their point of origin, sent to a port by
truck or railroad flatcar, and hoisted aboard a vessel specially
designed to carry as many as ten thousand so-called cans. Containers awaiting shipment do not need warehouses; they are
stacked up on paved areas that resemble vast parking lots. Nor
does loading and unloading rely on a large pool of longshore-
men, since the work is largely automated. The great advantage
of container shipping is the efficient transfer of cargo from one
mode of transportation to another, so direct access to highways
and railroad lines is essential. The old urban ports, surrounded
by dense residential neighborhoods and narrow streets, were ill
suited to handling the transshipment of containers, and it was
far more efficient to build brand-new ports—containerports.

This technological change had a devastating effect on traditional port cities. As late as the mid-1950s, New York City had
283 working piers. In 1955, New Jersey announced that it was
building the largest containerport in the country, and within
five years it was handling more than half of the region's cargo.
By 1970, New York City was down to only one-fiftieth of the

tonnage it had a decade earlier, and most of the Manhattan and Brooklyn piers, including ones that had recently been refurbished (and would form the basis for Brooklyn Bridge Park), stood empty.[9] The same cycle was repeated in other maritime cities. Oakland took the majority of shipping business from San Francisco, as Seattle did from Portland. Unlike a traditional port, a containerport does not have to be close to a city. The old urban Port of New Orleans, for example, now handles chiefly cruise ships; its freight function has been replaced by the sprawling Port of South Louisiana, which stretches fifty miles from north of the city to as far as the outskirts of Baton Rouge.

Such momentous changes in how goods are transported left the old port cities with abandoned wharves and empty warehouses. What was to be done with this waterfront real estate? San Francisco showed the way. In 1962, William Roth, a local developer, purchased a two-and-a-half-acre waterfront site in the Fisherman's Wharf district from the Ghirardelli Chocolate Company, which was moving to a suburban location near the airport. Roth converted the old factory and warehouse into restaurants and shops, adding a raised pedestrian plaza that provided wonderful views of San Francisco Bay. Ghirardelli Square, as it was called, is not a historic restoration. The architects, Wurster, Bernardi & Emmons, gutted the old buildings and pragmatically added new structures, including a three-hundred-car garage. The result, as Alexander Garvin put it, "successfully combined nostalgia for old San Francisco with the freshness of a new retail facility."[10]

Ghirardelli Square proved immensely popular and spawned another project nearby. Leonard Martin, a developer, bought an empty three-story brick structure from the Del Monte com-

Ghirardelli Square in San Francisco
introduced a new urban-renewal formula:
rehabilitated waterfront buildings + commerce +
tourism = downtown activity.

pany, and architect Joseph Esherick transformed what had
been a peach cannery into The Cannery, a picturesque complex of art galleries, a comedy club, and a movie theater, as well
as a mixture of restaurants and shops. In less than a decade,
thanks to Ghirardelli Square and The Cannery, the Fisherman's Wharf district became one of the city's chief attractions.
Other public and private developments included a maritime
museum, berthed historic ships, and an amusement park on a

cargo pier, as well as Fisherman's Wharf itself, once the center of San Francisco's commercial fishing fleet and now a collection of waterside seafood restaurants.

Fisherman's Wharf is an example of successful revitalization based not on urban renewal, public housing, or grand civic projects, but on tourism. Tourism was largely ignored by the first generation of urban-renewal planners—even Jane Jacobs had nothing to say about it—but it proved to be a powerful economic force for urban change. Cities that couldn't recover lost manufacturing and industrial jobs discovered something that older European cities such as Venice and Vienna had known for a long time: instead of offering financial services or manufacturing shoes, a city could sell pleasure.

Unlike the failed urban-renewal projects of the 1960s, Ghirardelli Square and The Cannery were a hit with the public. This was in no small part due to their designs; Wurster's and Esherick's architecture, refreshingly unpolemical in a relaxed Northern Californian manner, is an eclectic mixture of old and new. Rather than remaking the city in a Utopian image, or adapting a model from the suburbs, these architects took advantage of precisely those attractive attributes that were unique to cities: interesting-looking, old industrial buildings, vibrant density, and, above all, the unique character of a waterfront.

Ghirardelli Square and The Cannery were private development projects, but an earlier Texas waterfront-improvement project followed a different model: public funding in the first phase and private initiative in the second. The city of San Antonio, founded in 1718, sits athwart the winding San Antonio River, and like most North American cities, it has historically treated the river merely as a commercial convenience. By the

Urban infrastructure transformed into a recreation site
in San Antonio's secluded Paseo del Rio.

early 1900s, no longer used for barge traffic, the river—which
is a dozen feet below street level—had become an unsightly
garbage dump. In 1926, after a disastrous downtown flood, city
engineers proposed redirecting the watercourse into an underground conduit. Construction was stopped after a number of
public meetings, and influenced by a proposal by local architect Robert Hugman, the city decided to undertake a civic beautification project instead. In 1938–41, with the support of the
federal Works Progress Administration, floodgates and a bypass
channel were built, and the horseshoe-shaped river, flanked by
ancient bald cypress trees, was transformed into a linear park
with walkways along the riverbanks.[11] Thirty-one new stair-
ways led down from the street, and twenty-one new pedestrian

bridges crossed the watercourse. Hugman had called his original proposal "The Shops of Aragon and Romula." That name didn't stick—the linear park was christened Paseo del Rio—but his vision of shops and restaurants along a picturesque waterside promenade came to fruition, and the Paseo, or River Walk, became a popular and commercial success. Like Ghirardelli Square, the Paseo was also a tourist attraction capitalizing on nostalgia, in this case for the city's Spanish heritage, which was alluded to in Hugman's design for the staircases and bridges. During the 1960s, the Paseo was twice enlarged; in 1968 a waterway was extended to the new convention center, and a major hotel, the Hilton Palacio del Rio, was added to the commercial mix.*

The lessons of the Paseo del Rio and Ghirardelli Square were soon applied elsewhere. In Boston, the Redevelopment Authority was looking for a commercial use for the city-owned Quincy Market, three historic waterfront buildings that had served as a public market since 1826 but were now empty. In 1974, James Rouse, a Baltimore-based shopping-center builder, was designated the developer of the six-and-a-half-acre site. The floor area of the old market was 370,000 square feet, equivalent to a small regional shopping center, and enough office workers and residents were within walking distance of the site to support stores and restaurants, but Rouse decided to target tourists as well as locals. Instead of building anchor stores, he created a retail center that consisted only of small, primarily local, businesses—160 of them—including shops and restaurants, and, in

*In 1981, another branch was built as far as the Alamo, and there is talk today of extending what is now a network of canals north and south of the city.

the outdoor areas, scores of pushcarts. Rouse's architect, Benjamin Thompson, added glass extensions to the main central building, creating a shopping place whose architecture combined the old and the new. Thompson made the public spaces narrow, emphasizing density and pedestrian activity; the upper floors of the old market were turned into offices. In another departure from convention, no parking was provided.

Like Ghirardelli Square, Quincy Market is a commercial development that attracts the public through its iconoclastic approach to urban development, and like Paseo del Rio it is a successful partnership of public and private interests. Rouse and Thompson went on to build a second so-called festival marketplace on Baltimore's Inner Harbor. Though smaller than Quincy Market, and lacking historical structures, Harborplace was equally successful, and annual sales in both developments exceeded those of traditional suburban shopping malls. The festival marketplace model has been repeated in several cities, by Rouse and others: New York's South Street Seaport, Miami's Bayside Marketplace, and Chicago's Navy Pier. While more formulaic, and often considerably less charming, than their predecessors, all capitalize on the same simple fact: people like to be near water.

8

* ▪ ▣ ▪ *

The Bilbao Anomaly

A watershed event in the history of American city planning occurred in 1956 when the University of Pennsylvania inaugurated a joint degree program in city planning and architecture. The goal was to educate professionals who could bridge the gap that had grown up between city planners, who were increasingly concerned with large-scale urban policy, and architects, who tended to focus on individual buildings. Henry Wright, the former partner of Clarence Stein and the codesigner of Radburn, helped draft the proposal: "The need, the urgent need, now exists for a designer with a broad vision, with understanding of the life of the city and these times, and above all with unusual skill in composing buildings in relation to each other and to their natural setting and to the activities of the city."[1] The new discipline came to be known as urban design.* Urban designers deal with collections of buildings, such as downtown

*The 1956 planning conference at which Jane Jacobs had spoken against urban renewal led Harvard to establish a degree in urban design in 1959.

business districts, residential neighborhoods, planned communities, town centers, and college campuses. While they are often architects, urban designers don't design individual buildings. Instead, they plan the public spaces between buildings — avenues, streets, squares, promenades, and parks — and establish general guidelines, such as setbacks, heights, and other rules that govern how buildings relate to one another. Reacting to the failures of the megaprojects of the 1950s — and to Jane Jacobs's critique — urban designers recognize that building a city is different from constructing a building; in this gradual process, many actors participate over long periods of time.[2] Thus, the goal of an urban-design plan is to create a loose framework that will accommodate this process, acknowledging that the future is usually impossible to predict. On the whole, this approach has proved workable and useful, as Harborplace and Reston Town Center demonstrate.

A different sort of watershed occurred on July 20, 2002, during a town-hall meeting held at the Javits Convention Center in New York City. The meeting was organized by the Civic Alliance to Rebuild Downtown New York, a coalition of community groups; the subject was the reconstruction of the World Trade Center site in the wake of the September 11 terrorist attacks the previous year. The Lower Manhattan Development Corporation, which is responsible for the rebuilding, presented a number of urban-design schemes showing how 11 million square feet of offices, retail space, a hotel, and a memorial to the victims could be arranged on the sixteen-acre site. The drawings and models were the work of Beyer Blinder Belle, a New York architecture and planning firm that designed the South Street Seaport Museum and recently turned Stone Street in Lower

Manhattan into a successful outdoor restaurant row. However, only two of the schemes presented at the Javits Center were designed by Beyer Blinder Belle; two were the work of Peterson Littenberg, an architecture and planning firm that espoused New Urbanism; one was based on a plan that the powerhouse architects Skidmore, Owings & Merrill had prepared for Larry Silverstein, the leaseholder of the destroyed Twin Towers; and the sixth was based on a master plan designed by Alexander Cooper, one of the designers of Battery Park City.

The authors of the six alternatives were not given an opportunity to speak at the town-hall meeting. Instead, the projects were presented to the public in the form of what urban designers call massing models, which represent generic building volumes and lack specific architectural details. The forty-five hundred people who attended the meeting broke up into small discussion groups that were electronically connected to a central database, allowing instant polling of the attendees. It quickly became apparent from the tabulated reactions that the audience didn't like any of the proposals. The common complaints were that the architecture was unimaginative, that there were too many office buildings, and that the memorial areas were not inspiring. In sum, the Development Corporation was seen as having fallen down on the job. When Robert Yaro, one of the Civic Alliance's founders, offered conciliatory remarks, he was shouted down by the assembly. The vociferous reactions to the plans echoed a *New York Times* lead editorial of three days earlier titled "The Downtown We Don't Want," which described the six schemes as "dreary, leaden proposals that fall far short of what New York City—and the world—expect to see rise at ground zero."[3] Portentous prose, but an accurate reflection of the public mood.

Obviously, there was a disconnect between the urban design-ers and the public. The former saw rebuilding the World Trade Center site as a technical problem—which streets to close and which to open, where to build, how to accommodate compli-cated underground infrastructure, and how to deal with trans-portation (streets, subways, and a PATH line). The urban designers intentionally avoided superblock solutions and dif-fidently aimed at reintegrating the World Trade Center site with the rest of the city. As Paul Goldberger, the architecture critic of the *New Yorker,* put it at the time, "Boldness has been pretty much out of fashion in city-planning circles for a while, especially in lower Manhattan, where it is associated not only with projects like the World Trade Center but with unrealized schemes like the expressway Robert Moses wanted to run across downtown, which would have destroyed SoHo."[4] But bold-ness was what the public wanted. It saw the reconstruction of Ground Zero not as a chance to repair the city but as an oppor-tunity to create new, exciting architectural forms that would, in some as yet undefined way, both symbolize and commemorate the events of 9/11.

Even before the town-hall meeting was over, the cowed officials of the Lower Manhattan Development Corporation announced that they would extend the deadline for completing a final master plan in order to consider fresh options.[5] The six urban-design proposals were shelved, and a month later an inter-national competition for "conceptual ideas" was announced. Four hundred and six teams responded, and seven were selected. Some of the team members had planning experience, but most were high-profile architects, among them two Pritzker Prize win-ners—Richard Meier and Norman Foster—such well-known designers as Charles Gwathmey, Rafael Viñoly, Peter Eisenman, and Steven Holl, and younger international architects such as Daniel Libeskind, lately of Berlin, Foreign Office Architects of London, and UNStudio of Amsterdam.

The earlier urban-design proposals had taken into account such mundane factors as subway stations, transit lines, existing river tunnels, and underground infrastructure, as well as connections to Battery Park City on the west and Tribeca on the north. The new projects generally downplayed these constraints and concentrated on architectural form: Foster designed an unusual pair of connected skyscrapers; the team of Meier, Eisenman, Holl, and Gwathmey produced a striking composition of five identical towers; Libeskind placed his buildings around a huge memorial excavation; and the team that included Foreign Office Architects and UNStudio proposed a colossal megastructure of a type that had never been built before—and was, perhaps, unbuildable. Although architecture critics generally praised the results, not everyone was pleased. "It is like putting lipstick on a hog," complained Yaro. "Nothing has changed except you have a lot of fancy architects on this go-round. They are still designing the same thing, just prettier."[6] He meant that the program had not changed and still consisted primarily of office buildings.* But his criticism missed the point: fancy architects and pretty models were precisely what the public—egged on by the media, especially the *New York Times*—wanted.

That is why the Javits Center town meeting was a milestone.

---

*The Port Authority, which owns the World Trade Center site, is prohibited by law from building housing.

Forty years earlier, Jane Jacobs had criticized city planning for "sorting out certain cultural or public functions and decontaminating their relationship with the workaday city."[7] The new discipline of urban design was a response to her critique, but the public would have none of it. In the words of architect and author Philip Nobel, "The universal negative reaction that would kill the plans was not only a knee-jerk response to unsatisfying architecture . . . it marked the death of reasoned planning at Ground Zero."[8]

The rejection of urban design in favor of showcase architecture was influenced by a major phenomenon of the late 1990s: the public's fascination with so-called signature or iconic buildings, that is, striking buildings designed by architectural stars. Emblematic architecture in cities is not new, of course. European urbanism in the second half of the nineteenth century, for example, included massive railroad terminals, palatial department stores, huge exhibition halls, and impressive opera houses, not to mention urban landmarks such as the Eiffel Tower. Historian Barry Bergdoll characterizes this period as embodying the "cult of the monument" and links the rise of officially sanctioned and historically inspired architecture in Europe to the rise of nationalist ideologies in new states such as Germany, Belgium, and Italy, and to the growing power of commercial interests.[9] "Belatedly architecture joined the arsenal of the burgeoning art of advertising," he writes, "which quickly exploited even the newest findings of the young field of visual psychology to fine-tune its message and appeal."[10] The connection between architecture and advertising was particularly evident in the entrepreneurial United States, where the first four decades of the twentieth century witnessed a veritable explosion of commercial monuments: hotels and apartment buildings in the form of aristocratic châteaus, railroad stations modeled on Roman baths, department stores resembling Florentine palazzi, and those most visible of urban monuments, commercial skyscrapers.

The public's appetite for striking architecture, in any period, is fueled by similar forces: prosperity, civic ambition, confidence in the future, and a sense that one's own epoch is unique and needs its own form of special expression. The first postwar building to achieve the status of an instant national icon was the Sydney Opera House, designed by the Danish architect Jørn Utzon and completed in 1973. Despite its relatively remote location—most non-Australians did not see the Opera House firsthand until the 2000 Olympic Games—the sculptural concrete roofs and the spectacular site captured the world's imagination. Charles Jencks, the author of *The Iconic Building*, describes architectural icons as delicate balancing acts between what he calls explicit signs and implicit symbols, that is, between memorable forms and the images they conjure up. He emphasizes that in an increasingly heterogeneous world, multiple and sometimes even enigmatic meanings are precisely what turn buildings into popular icons. According to Jencks, the billowing white roofs of the Opera House could be read as sails, waves, or seashells.[11] This has little to do with music, but it seems just right for Sydney Harbor and Australia.

In 1991, when Frank Gehry entered an international competition to design a new Guggenheim Museum in Bilbao, Spain, his clients referred specifically to the Sydney Opera House. "It

An architectural icon as the catalyst for urban renewal.

was a small competition with Arata Isozaki, Coop Himmelblau, and me and they—Thomas Krens [the director of the Guggenheim Museum] and the Basques—said they needed a hit there," Gehry told Charles Jencks. "They needed the building to do for Bilbao what the Sydney Opera House did for Australia."[12] Gehry delivered. Since its opening, the museum has attracted more than 4 million visitors to the city and generated millions of dollars of economic activity and new taxes for the city. It has transformed Bilbao from an aging industrial port into a prime tourist destination. While other constructions—an improved subway system, a new airport, a shopping complex—have contributed to the city's rejuvenation, the Guggenheim Museum deserves the lion's share of the credit.

As with the Sydney Opera House, the symbolism of the Bilbao museum is enigmatic. The titanium swirls, ballooning shapes, and colliding forms have variously been described as biomorphic sculpture and an intergalactic spaceship; locally it's known as the silver artichoke. Whatever its meaning, Gehry's museum has had a major impact on contemporary architecture, pushing design in an expressionistic, sculptural direction. It has also influenced the way that many architects, and their clients, think about urbanism. "A single piece of architecture can be a more effective catalyst for change than a corps of urban planners," says New York architect Steven Holl, neatly if somewhat arrogantly summarizing what has come to be known as the Bilbao Effect—the ability of a work of architecture to single-handedly put a city on the map.[13] As cities increasingly depend on national and international tourism, publicity has become important in attracting visitors. Whether it is a concert hall or a rock-and-roll hall of fame, a building that garners attention is an added reason for people to visit a city.

Although the Bilbao Effect assumes that buildings become icons overnight, history suggests otherwise. The Eiffel Tower, for example, was hardly universally popular when it was first built; and the tower housing Big Ben, which was built in 1852, achieved its iconic status during the London Blitz. When the Chrysler Building was built, it was vilified by most architecture critics as gaudy and commercialized, and during the Depression, the half-leased Empire State Building was ridiculed as the "Empty State."[14] Unpopular buildings may become popular in time, but as fashions change, the opposite can also happen. When Philadelphia decided to build a spectacular new city hall in 1871, the architect John McArthur Jr. chose the ornate Second Empire style, which was then the height of fashion. However, it took so long to build the enormous structure that by the time it was finished, thirty years later, tastes had changed. Beaux Arts classicism was all the rage, and the city hall's mansard roofs and florid decorations struck most people as old-fashioned, if not downright dowdy. The vast stone pile became something of an embarrassment, and calls to demolish the building started as early as the 1920s and continued for decades. Probably only its size — it is the largest municipal building in the United States — saved it from the wrecker's ball. By the 1980s, tastes had again changed. Thanks to the historic-preservation movement, old buildings in general, and Victorian architecture in particular, were seen as architectural assets. In the 2007 poll that asked Americans to rate their favorite buildings, the city hall stood in twenty-first place, just behind the Brooklyn Bridge and ahead of any other building in Philadelphia.[15]

Buildings of far greater architectural worth than Philadelphia's city hall have not weathered the shoals of changing taste. Charles McKim's epic Pennsylvania Station was demolished fifty-four years after it opened; Frank Lloyd Wright's splendid Larkin Building was gone after forty-seven years; H. H. Richardson's monumental Marshall Field store endured forty-three years; and Stanford White's marvelous Madison Square Garden was taken down after only twenty-five. The hardest test for a building is between its thirtieth and fiftieth birthdays, when architectural tastes have changed and the original design no longer seems fresh. That is when calls for demolition — or drastic alterations — are most likely to be heeded. If a building weathers this midlife crisis, after several more decades, as the pendulum of fashion swings back, it may once more be appreciated. It helps if a building is functionally, as well as aesthetically, outstanding, for the argument that great architecture should be held to a different practical standard generally falls on deaf ears. It also helps if a building captures people's affections. It is not enough that a building be popular with the general public, however; it must also be appreciated by its owner. If an owner values a building, he will put up with a certain degree of dysfunction—no building is perfect—and will take the trouble to maintain it, make repairs, upgrade obsolete technological systems, and spruce it up every thirty to forty years. If a building fails to capture its owner's favor, however, even architectural greatness will not protect it from the wrecker's ball.

The Bilbao Guggenheim is barely a decade old, so it is much too early to know how its idiosyncratic architectural style will age, aesthetically and functionally, although its current popularity is incontestable. However, the Bilbao Effect might be better named the Bilbao Anomaly, since it has proved difficult to replicate. Hot on the heels of Gehry's spectacular success in Bilbao, for example, the Microsoft billionaire Paul Allen commissioned Gehry to design a rock-and-roll museum for Seattle. The Experience Music Project was to commemorate the rock guitarist Jimi Hendrix, a Seattle native, and put the city, whose only memorable building was the Space Needle, on the architectural map. However, the much anticipated building turned out to be a dud, a jumble of forms, materials, and colors that tried too hard to be a literal representation of rock and roll (the shapes were said to have been inspired by electric guitars). Whether it was the confusing architecture, the lackluster contents, or some flaw in iconic chemistry, the Bilbao Effect failed to work its magic. Attendance was considerably less than expected, staff was let go, and in a hapless effort to attract the public, part of the building was turned into a Science Fiction Museum and Hall of Fame.

Describing the fate of most post-Bilbao museums, the *New York Times* warns, "The good news is that for a year after the opening of a new building, a major spike in attendance can be expected. The bad news is that attendance consistently levels off after two or three years."[16] Sometimes it doesn't even take that long. The new addition to the Denver Art Museum, designed by Studio Daniel Libeskind, was expected to attract 1 million visitors, and instead the first year it brought in 650,000; as a result, the museum has been obliged to lay off staff.[17] Steven Holl's ambitious claim for architecture's ascendancy over city planning was made in reference to his design for a new art museum in Bellevue, outside Seattle. That museum was intended to spearhead change in the lifeless downtown. "Holl hopes viewers will see architecture as an urban amenity, one that is beautiful even as it connects people—a first step in the utopian transformation of an edge city," breathlessly opined *Architectural Record*.[18] Less than three years after it opened, and following the resignations of two successive directors, the Bellevue Arts Museum closed its doors because of "failure to find an audience."[19]

In 1987, Philadelphia decided to build a new downtown concert hall. Since the budget was only $60 million—low for a concert hall—Robert Venturi designed a straightforward brick box, almost an anti-icon. Asked to make the building more "interesting," the architect cheekily added neon decorations to the façade. By then, the Bilbao Effect was much on people's minds, the general feeling was that something more was called for, and Venturi was let go. Following an architectural competition, the job went to Rafael Viñoly, who produced an unusual design with two halls under an enormous glass roof. The coverage of the building in the national media was decidedly tepid, however, especially compared to the plaudits that greeted Gehry's Walt Disney Hall in Los Angeles, which opened the same year.

The Bilbao Effect failed to work its magic
at the Bellevue Arts Museum.

Shortly after Philadelphia's Kimmel Center was completed, the management took the unusual step of suing its architect, ostensibly for cost overruns and construction delays, but according to the *Philadelphia Inquirer*, "the underlying complaint seems to be that Viñoly failed to deliver a show-stopper."[20]

The demands of the public may forge the shape of cities, as Andrejs Skaburskis pointed out, but with the Bilbao Effect these demands often have negative consequences. In the past, civic monuments, since they were to last not decades but centuries, were expected to exhibit gravity and decorum. Buildings such as the New York Public Library and Washington's Union Station were intended to impress and even dazzle, but they were not expected to astonish or entertain. Since today's architectural icons are competing for attention not only with one another, but also with such public distractions as movies, music videos, and computer games, architects—and their clients—have waived all restraint. Aggressively pursuing novelty, architects have explored increasingly bizarre forms and unusual materials and have striven for surprising spatial and structural effects. But while fireworks are wonderful, who wants fireworks every night?

The public's demand for novelty has distorted not only architecture but also urban design. Intensely self-centered buildings usually make poor urban neighbors, and a city of icons risks becoming the architectural equivalent of a theme park—or the Las Vegas strip.* The Bilbao Guggenheim succeeded because it is a brilliant crystal in a staid setting of sturdy nineteenth-century buildings. Successful examples of urban design, such as seventeenth-century Amsterdam, Georgian Edinburgh and London, and nineteenth-century Paris, are similarly characterized by the quality of their streets and squares—and canals—and the orderly beauty of their everyday buildings. The real challenge for cities today is not to create more icons, but rather to create more such settings. The current economic recession may aid in this, since funding for large projects has dried up and economic conditions favor modest initiatives—repairing, rehabilitating, and reusing buildings rather than tearing them down and starting over.

Were the participants at the 2002 Javits Center town-hall meeting hoping for some local version of the Bilbao Effect?

---

*Icon overload is already visible in cities such as Dubai and Shanghai.

Daniel Libeskind's winning scheme, which has been described as a "shrine to patriotism," pointedly included a number of iconic elements: a 1,776-foot-high skyscraper, a Heroes Park, a September 11 Place, and a public plaza oriented to receive a shaft of sunlight each September 11—the so-called Wedge of Light.[21] Many people were taken by the design. "Build Mr. Libeskind's memorial, it will be a source and incubator of renewal," wrote Ada Louise Huxtable in the *Wall Street Journal*, anticipating a Bilbao Effect.[22] But we will never know. After Libeskind's design had gone through the ringer of engineering constraints, real-estate economics, and political infighting, virtually all its symbolic elements, including the memorial slurry wall, an immense waterfall, and a shardlike museum, disappeared. If Ground Zero was to have an icon, it looked as if it might be the new PATH commuter train station being designed by Santiago Calatrava, who produced one of his characteristic avian skeletons with a vast openable roof. But that project is encountering a common problem of putative icons: high construction costs, in this case in excess of $3 *billion*.[23] At the time of writing—fall 2010—as redesign follows redesign (the roof no longer opens), it is not clear what form the final station will take.

Yet the World Trade Center site *is* being rebuilt. The new 7 World Trade Center, which includes an all-important electrical substation, is occupied. The underground infrastructure is nearing completion; a design has been chosen for the memorial; construction of 1 World Trade Center, an eighty-two-story skyscraper designed by David Childs and Skidmore, Owings & Merrill, has begun; and Richard Rogers, Norman Foster, and Fumihiko Maki have been commissioned to design three adjacent office towers. The final Ground Zero plan is striking for how much it resembles one of the urban-design proposals that was so publicly rejected in 2002: the Alexander Cooper plan. Only two weeks after 9/11, Cooper, Robertson & Partners was commissioned to make a study of the area by Brookfield Properties, which owned the World Financial Center next door. The heart of Cooper's plan was restoring Greenwich and Fulton streets, eliminated when the World Trade Center was built in 1973, and creating a connection between lower Manhattan and the World Financial Center. To reinforce this connection, Cooper proposed decking over a section of ten-lane-wide West Street, creating a new, narrower avenue, as well as a treed pedestrian promenade that extended as far south as Battery Park on the tip of the island. The most expensive part of the plan was underground: a new Long Island Rail Road terminus for a high-speed line linking lower Manhattan to Jamaica in the suburbs. Restoring the two streets cut the sixteen-acre superblock into four parcels. Cooper pointed out that the largest of the four, which circumscribed the footprints of the two destroyed towers, was roughly the same size as Madison Square or Bryant Park and could serve as a memorial park.

The Cooper master plan successfully resolved the key issues of the World Trade Center site, and according to Cooper's partner Jaquelin T. Robertson, it acquired such an air of inevitability that it was "unofficially approved by the State, the City, and the Port Authority long before any redevelopment agency had been set up, and the various studies and fashion shows started." Although the new railroad line and the deck over West Street were ultimately set aside as too expensive, many of the components of the plan are being realized: the restored Greenwich

The 2002 Cooper, Robertson study established the main urban-design parameters for the World Trade Center site.

and Fulton streets, the office towers and a new station on the east side of Greenwich Street, and a memorial that incorporates the Twin Tower footprints. Libeskind's scheme proposed that the memorial parcel be thirty feet below street level, but the present memorial design is a street-level park, just as the Cooper plan proposed. This is not a question of copying. Cooper's plan, which is based on rational analysis rather than personal invention, simply anticipated the most sensible outcome. So perhaps urban design could be said to have prevailed at Ground Zero, after all.

9

Putting the Pieces Together

The World Trade Center site is an example of an abrupt and unanticipated need for urban redevelopment, but cities are always building and rebuilding to accommodate growing populations and technological and cultural changes. Perhaps the most common urban change is densification. Densification has many advantages: more people on the street (which usually offers a safer environment), more shops, more amenities, more choices, more efficient mass transit, higher property values. Densification also produces a larger municipal tax base, which is important for those cities that lost population when they deindustrialized during the postwar years. Thanks to deindustrialization, smaller households, and larger residential units, current population densities in cities, even in the densest cities, are still far below what they were a hundred years ago.[1] So, talk of "vertical sprawl," an alarmist term used by opponents of urban densification, is premature.[2]

Urban densification is not evenly spread across the city, however, but tends to occur in proximity to amenities such as downtowns, cultural districts, parks, and waterfronts. It is precisely density that allows these amenities to achieve their full potential. The success of a shopping street, a city park, or a waterfront esplanade depends on the presence of large numbers of people. An uninhabited street, a deserted park, or an empty esplanade are not only unattractive, they may even appear threatening and dangerous. So, in densification, which comes first, the amenities or the people?

"Build it and they will come" is one answer. Large mixed-use projects can prime the pump by attracting many residents in a relatively short time. Since sufficient amenities must be in place from the beginning to attract buyers and tenants, the success of such projects depends on developers who have the financial resources to fund the considerable up-front investment, the proverbial deep pockets. The project must have a large enough critical mass to warrant such investments, and the developer must have the experience and resources to deal with a variety of uses. The role of city government is important, particularly in land assembly and in facilitating community acceptance. Design is critical, too, since the project must quickly establish that elusive quality, *a sense of place*. To effectively prime a pump there must be water in the well, however; it is essential that the city be part of a growing and economically healthy metropolitan region. Downtown densification is not a recipe for saving declining cities.

The challenge for planners is how to jump-start development without falling into the pitfalls that plagued the large urban-renewal projects of the 1950s. This can be difficult, as the checkered history of Penn's Landing in Philadelphia demonstrates. The seventy-five-acre site on the Delaware River was created in the early 1960s with landfill from the construction of a sunken crosstown expressway. Penn's Landing, at the foot of Market Street and adjacent to downtown, was seen as a potentially lucrative development opportunity by the city, which owned the site, and the city department of commerce commissioned a master plan for the area. In the prevailing spirit of urban renewal, the development was conceived as a superblock, consisting of a landmark office tower housing the port authority, additional office space, a science park, and a boat basin. As part of a strategy to revitalize Philadelphia's role as a port, the plan included an embarcadero that could berth two thirty-thousand-ton cruise ships. The goal was to complete the project in time for a planned 1976 Philadelphia world's fair to coincide with the bicentennial of the signing of the Declaration of Independence.

The Penn's Landing plan, which captured the imagination of public officials, notably Edmund N. Bacon, executive director of the city's planning commission, contained a number of flaws. It was described as a logical extension of William Penn's original plan, but a little thought might have raised questions about the wisdom of locating office buildings two miles away from the existing business district. Moreover, access to the site was problematic. A major interstate highway, I-95, as yet unbuilt but in its final planning stages, would necessitate a four-hundred-foot-long overpass, making for a tenuous connection between Penn's Landing and the rest of the city.

Thanks to intensive lobbying by the city and the state, federal highway planners agreed to depress I-95 for the seven blocks opposite Penn's Landing, which at least allowed street-level access to the site. In 1970, a quasi-public body, the Penn's Landing Corporation, was founded, and three years later it announced a developer competition for a mixed-use project on the site. The winning entry consisted of three high-rise buildings containing offices, apartments, and a hotel, all sitting on top of a fourteen-hundred-foot-long parking structure (proximity to the river meant that parking had to be aboveground). The parking structure was required since most people were expected to come to Penn's Landing by car, and the developer requested that new ramps be added to I-95, which was then under construction. This produced vocal opposition from neighborhood groups, who feared increased local street traffic, and after several years of hearings, the ramp was voted down. As a consequence, the developer withdrew from the project.

The bicentennial was looming, and although the city had lost its bid to host a world's fair, $13 million was spent landscaping part of Penn's Landing to serve for special events such as fireworks and concerts, the first *public* uses on the site. The next twenty years saw four different proposals to develop the area. In one case, the city commissioned a master plan but could not identify a developer to implement it; in another, a slowdown in the national economy scuttled a mixed-use project. The Rouse company, in the wake of its successful waterfront projects in Boston and Baltimore, unveiled an ambitious design for a festival marketplace, but after losing an anchor tenant, Disney, and facing a nationwide slump in retailing, it canceled the project.

It was now more than thirty years since the first master plan for Penn's Landing, and all the proposals for complicated mixed-use projects had fallen through. Finally, in 1997, the city picked the Simon DeBartolo company to develop an entertainment and retail complex; in other words, a shopping mall.

A new feature of the site was a federally funded aerial tram connecting Penn's Landing to Camden, across the river. As the mall project developed over the next five years, construction costs spiraled from the original $130 million to $329 million. Then in 2002, as the economy weakened, Simon DeBartolo announced that it was withdrawing from the project. With the tram under construction, the city found itself in an embarrassing situation, and a new call for developer proposals was cobbled together. But after four unconvincing submissions, the project was shelved. All that remains are the pylons for the now defunct aerial tram.

It would be wrong to describe Penn's Landing merely as a development failure, since a number of new uses are in the area: low-rise housing on two abandoned piers, a hotel, a maritime museum, a skating rink, and a landscaped plaza that is the site of regular concerts, fireworks, and assorted public festivities. Nevertheless, the millions of dollars that were spent over the years on plans, public hearings, infrastructure improvements, and public institutions have not borne fruit.

The story of Penn's Landing shows the difficulties inherent in the wholesale development of large urban sites. Successful megaprojects, such as Rockefeller Center, are few and far between and are generally the result of unique circumstances (in that case, the Depression, which reduced construction costs, and an immensely wealthy client). The challenge for a site as large and isolated as Penn's Landing was that it needed a critical mass, but because of its size it took so long to implement that it was particularly susceptible to market cycles. Over and over, the plans ran into the reality of falling demand, yet the need to make a grand architectural gesture—inherited from Bacon's original master plan—prevented the city from scaling back the project to more realistic dimensions.

Penn's Landing also shows the thorny problem of combining public and private spaces in the city. The project started as private commercial development, then assumed a more public face. This produced confusion about the appropriate character of the place. Was it a public amenity that deserved the support of public funds? Or was it a commercial site that should depend on private financing? But if it was the latter, as in the case of the shopping mall, why were public subsidies required? To say that the project had to be both public and private merely blurred the distinction, both functionally and politically. Unlike Brooklyn Bridge Park, Penn's Landing never had a clear strategy for how to use private development to reinforce the public good.

The answer to large urban development has turned out to be big projects that are, at the same time, collections of little plans. Like Penn's Landing, Battery Park City on the Hudson River in Lower Manhattan was built on landfill (produced by the excavations for the World Trade Center). The ninety-two-acre project was planned and coordinated by the Battery Park City Authority, a public-benefit corporation created by New York State in 1968, about the same time as the Penn's Landing Corporation came into being. As in Philadelphia, the first designs for Battery Park City were ambitious megastructures on superblocks, and they suffered the same fate. The project took a different turn in 1979, when the Authority commissioned Alexander Cooper and Stanton Eckstut to create a plan that could be implemented by several different developers in successive phases. Cooper and

Eckstut extended the uneven Lower Manhattan street grid into the site, creating small parcels of land that could be filled in with medium- and high-rise apartment blocks.* Like Reston Town Center, Battery Park City was designed to grow piecemeal, building by building, with individual projects financed and built by different developers, in response to changing market demand, but following the architectural guidelines of the master plan. This approach was successful, and with the exception of the World Financial Center—a single-developer office complex in which all the buildings were designed by a single architect, Cesar Pelli—the physical results are pleasantly heterogeneous and avoid the architectural uniformity that so bedeviled earlier urban-renewal projects.

Battery Park City includes a variety of shops, several public schools, restaurants, hotels, museums, a multiscreen movie theater, and a yacht basin. The development, which will ultimately house sixty thousand residents and office workers, demonstrates how a public body can successfully work with private developers.[3] The mixed-use plan also shows that a return to a more traditional urbanism is not only feasible and financially viable, but also popular. The waterfront location of Battery Park City is a big part of this popularity. A mile-long public esplanade at the river's edge—the first in Manhattan—attracts visitors from outside the development and provides the requisite sense of place.

One of the largest examples of urban densification is Stapleton, a forty-seven-hundred-acre development on the site of Den-

---

*Battery Park City was separated from Lower Manhattan by the West Side Highway. Plans to put the elevated highway underground were canceled in 1985, and although the elevated structure was dismantled, eight-lane West Street remains a formidable barrier to pedestrians.

The attraction of water at the esplanade
in Battery Park City, New York.

ver's old airport, about fifteen minutes from downtown. Begun
in 2001 and developed by Forest City, a Cleveland-based developer that specializes in large urban projects, Stapleton will
have thirty thousand residents and thirty-five thousand new jobs
when it is complete. While consisting predominantly of single-
family housing, it also includes apartments and condominiums
and has a density of about twenty people per acre, compared to
a typical suburban density of ten people per acre. Surrounded
by existing urban neighborhoods, Stapleton has been able to
support more extensive retail and commercial uses, as well as
employment, than would have been possible in a suburban site.

Smaller (but denser) than Stapleton is Atlantic Station in
midtown Atlanta, on a 138-acre site that once housed a steel

In Stapleton, Denver, traditional main-street activities
animate a new neighborhood center.

mill. The project of local developer James F. Jacoby was begun
in 1998 and will contain five thousand residential units (both
high-rise apartments and single-family houses), 6 million square
feet of office space, 2 million square feet of retail space, and one
thousand hotel rooms, as well as a mixed-use town center—
in all, employment for thirty thousand people.[4] The commercial area, which consists mainly of four- and five-story buildings,
apartments and offices above stores, with streets and sidewalks,
is compact and walkable. The crisp modern design of the buildings, with restaurants and cafés spilling out onto the sidewalk,
reminded me of a new shopping district in Holland or Germany.

Equally modern is the architecture of a mixed-use development planned for downtown Washington, D.C., by developer Gerald Hines. Here, the old urban-renewal planning process will, in effect, be reversed. Starting with a superblock—which had been created in the 1970s to house a now demolished convention center—the planners, Foster + Partners, have reopened the old streets, carved the site up into six smaller blocks, and created an interior pedestrian shopping street where an alley historically existed. Integrated with its urban surroundings, the complex contains office buildings, condominiums, and apartment blocks, all with shopping at street level. A typical piece of downtown fabric, except that the buildings sit on top of a massive underground garage.

Denver, Atlanta, and Washington, D.C., are metropolitan regions that have experienced vigorous population growth, but not all cities have a sufficiently dynamic real estate market to attract large investments of capital (more than $5 billion in the case of Stapleton), or sufficient vacant land for large downtown projects. That doesn't mean that densification can't happen, but it will be smaller in scale and slower. In older cities, densification often means the conversion of disused industrial and commercial buildings to residential use. The process generally begins with small developers, entrepreneurs, and individuals who are prepared to take risks. Eventually, new residents attract small-scale retail, which in turn attracts more residents, perhaps young professionals and empty nesters. The growing demand encourages larger, better-financed developers to undertake larger projects, which bring with them more retail and entertainment venues, and so on. Although, in most cases, the initial decision to densify a neighborhood is taken by the market, not by public officials, the role of government is key, especially in the early phases. Facilitating permitting allows redevelopment to start at a small scale; tax abatements and historic preservation credits can provide incentives in weak markets; and in later phases, streetscape and infrastructure improvements and parks will attract more residents. Finally, constructing new public buildings such as libraries and schools, while it is unlikely to jump-start the process, can be an important reinforcement in later stages of development.

The Yards in Washington, D.C., a large waterfront development that combines residential, commercial, shopping, and recreational uses with historic buildings, is a good example of what city officials, developers, planners, and architects have learned about successfully infilling, restoring, and densifying urban districts. The site is at the foot of Capitol Hill in the near Southeast district of the city and occupies land that once belonged to the Washington Navy Yard. The historic shipbuilding yard and ordnance plant, founded in 1898, occupied 127 acres on the Anacostia River. In 1962, as naval ship construction was relocated elsewhere, half of the yard was decommissioned, and the land and buildings were transferred to the General Services Administration, or GSA, the agency responsible for managing the federal government's buildings and real estate. The GSA's plan was to create a campus of federal office buildings, but due to lack of funds, and a lack of interest on the part of federal agencies, only the Department of Transportation headquarters was built. In 2000, Congress gave the GSA special authority to sell or lease the rest of the site, forty-two acres, or to undertake a joint development with the private sector. In an unusual deci-

New development restores old buildings, adds new ones,
and creates waterside public parks at the Yards in Washington, D.C.

sion, the GSA chose the last course and signed a seventeen-year
agreement with developer Forest City Washington to create a
$1.7 billion mixed-use waterfront project where eighteen thou-
sand people will live and work.

The first phase of the Yards will be finished by 2010, and the
entire development will take another decade to complete. The
master plan, designed by Robert A. M. Stern Architects, Sha-
lom Baranes Associates, and SMWM, reintroduces the original streets and alleys, some of which had been closed by the
navy, and extends New Jersey Avenue, one of L'Enfant's diagonals, into the site, terminating it by a new treed square. The lessons of Reston Town Center and Battery Park City are evident
throughout: the streets cut the site up into relatively small parcels, allowing the developer to engage different architects for

the thirty different buildings. Architectural diversity is further assured by the presence of a 1915 Beaux Arts–style city pumping station, and several historic Navy Yard buildings: a large 1919 boilermaker's shop that will be reused for shopping and restaurants, and three industrial blocks that will be converted to residential use. In accordance with Washington's height restriction, the new buildings at the Yards are roughly ten stories high, many with shops at street level. The style of the new construction could best be described as "industrial chic": lots of glass, exposed concrete, and brick. Beside the river is a six-acre park, designed by the noted landscape architect Paul Friedberg, which incorporates a variety of activities: a boardwalk and a boat dock at the water's edge, a large lawn for public events, intimate gardens, and waterfalls and fountains, as well as hard surfaces near a historic structure that is turned into a restaurant pavilion, and new retail buildings that create a small festival marketplace. While the pedestrian mall idea of the 1970s has not been resurrected, Water Street, immediately behind the park, can selectively be closed to traffic for community events such as street fairs and farmers' markets.

The Yards demonstrates much of what has been learned about city building in the last three decades. The first lesson is that it is a mistake to ignore centuries of urban history. Old, well-tried planning solutions are often still the best: streets with sidewalks, street trees, individual buildings, a close mixture of different uses such as apartments above shops, and office buildings next to condominiums.

The second lesson is that while modern technology, whether it is the automobile or the Internet, can be a powerful force for change, new technology does not automatically require the city to be reinvented. In most cases, it is best simply to add another layer to the many layers of the past. Successful examples of urban interventions, such as Ghirardelli Square and Quincy Market, have involved adjustment rather than radical change—the conversion of old industrial buildings and the reconfiguration of obsolete waterfronts. Preserving history when it is possible and reinforcing the past are important. A further advantage of adjustment and preservation is that they help create a rich and distinctive sense of place.

The third lesson, derived from Jane Jacobs, is that urban amenities such as streets and parks work best when they are intensively used—one of the keys to urban vitality is density.* The residential population of the Yards will be nine thousand people, or more than two hundred people per acre; less than the three hundred people per acre at Battery Park City (which has apartment buildings as high as forty stories), but much denser than most urban neighborhoods outside Manhattan. Like Battery Park City, the Yards will also have a large number of office workers. Equally important is that the Yards is not conceived as an isolated "project," but rather as an integral part of the surrounding city. It is sandwiched between Nationals Park, a new forty-one-thousand-seat baseball stadium, and a working naval facility and is connected to the Anacostia Riverwalk Trail, an important regional amenity. This pragmatic combination of uses flies in the face of traditional planning-by-zoning, yet it will undoubtedly make the Yards a lively neighborhood. Like Battery Park City, the Yards is not a tourist attraction, but Wash-

*Conversely, even well-designed amenities will fail without sufficient users.

Mixing apartment and office buildings with ground-floor
retail contributes to urban vitality.

ingtonians will be drawn to the waterside park and its adjacent
restaurants (a Metro station is nearby).

One important way in which the Yards forms an integral part
of the city is in its proximity to modestly priced homes. In the
1940s and 1950s, Arthur Capper and Carrollsburg Dwellings,
a seven-hundred-unit public housing project, was built across
the street from the Washington Navy Yard. Like many housing
projects, this one suffered severe deterioration. The District of
Columbia Housing Authority, working with Forest City Washington and Urban Atlantic, a developer specializing in social
housing, demolished all the derelict housing on the thirty-five-
acre site and replaced it with a much denser development of
townhomes and apartment buildings, as well as a community

center, three office buildings, and stores. The houses are on tree-lined streets; the low-rise apartment buildings face a park. Capper/Carrollsburg is a HOPE VI project, a federal housing assistance program to cities that was begun in 1992. The goal of the program, according to the Department of Housing and Urban Development, is to "end the physical, social, and economic isolation of obsolete and severely distressed public housing by recreating and supporting sustainable communities and lifting residents from dependence and persistent poverty."[5] Unlike traditional public housing projects, HOPE VI developments are public-private partnerships in which social and market-rate housing are side by side.

Some HOPE VI projects have been criticized for substituting market housing for social housing, but the rebuilt Capper/Carrollsburg development replaces all the original housing units with rented public housing (including senior housing) and "workforce" housing, affordable for working families (restricted to households earning a stated percentage of the area's median income). In addition, the development adds nine hundred units in apartments and townhomes that are rented or sold at market prices. To deinstitutionalize the public housing, all the units—social, workforce, and market-rate—are built and managed by the private sector, rather than by a municipal housing agency. To further remove the stigma traditionally associated with "the projects," the social and market-rate units are indistinguishable.* Combining social and market-rate housing allowed the housing agency to leverage a $35 million

---

*The exteriors are identical; the interiors vary, since the market-rate units may have upgraded materials and finishes, depending on the buyers' preferences.

federal grant into $200 million of new public housing, as well as half a billion dollars of private development. The financial cross-subsidy is the result of building commercial and retail buildings as well as housing on the same site.

The lesson of Capper/Carrollsburg is an implicit critique of earlier public housing policies. No more superblocks, no more high-rise apartment buildings (most of the social housing will be in town houses or low-rise walk-ups), no more islands of concentrated poverty. In Capper/Carrollsburg, as in many other HOPE VI developments, social and market-rate units are side by side. This approach acknowledges that the design of the urban environment, both buildings and neighborhoods, must meet the market test. People's demands and desires, including those of poor people, must be taken into account.

The final lesson of the Yards is that the role of government in supporting urbanization remains important. The GSA as the client ensured the proper preservation and restoration of historic buildings, demanded the provision of well-designed public spaces, reviewed architectural guidelines, and oversaw the design and maintenance of public amenities. The HOPE VI project was similarly a collaboration of public and private interests. Such collaboration is complementary: developers are good at understanding what people want, but they tend to be focused on their own projects and are less interested in how these projects fit into—and affect—the surrounding city. Government, on the other hand, has not shown itself to be effective at city planning, often being more concerned with dictating what is "good for people" rather than discovering "what people want." Burdened by entrenched bureaucracies, government is also not good at responding to changing consumer demands. But a municipal government has the resources and the responsibility to deal with citywide issues such as infrastructure, transportation, and community concerns. Large urban projects definitely need to be planned, and successful planning requires public participation as well as private entrepreneurship.

10

The Kind of Cities We Want

"You can't have a society without cities," Edward G. Rendell, the mayor of Philadelphia, told an annual meeting of the Wharton Real Estate Center. It was 1996, and the mayor had just been reelected to a second term. He was known for never turning down an invitation to speak, whether to address a social gala or a neighborhood cookout, and especially not a chance to pitch his city to a roomful of developers, investors, and real estate mavens. Rendell spoke about his, and Philadelphia's, recent record in cutting costs and trimming the municipal bureaucracy. He ruefully admitted that on the basis of pure economics his city still had difficulty competing with the surrounding suburbs, but he appealed to the real estate industry's better nature. He pleaded—"We need your help." He cajoled—"We can do business together." He threatened—"We can't afford to ignore urban poverty." Rendell is an effective orator, with a raspy voice that adds to his eloquence. But he closed on an air of what appeared to be resignation: "We can't simply let our cities decline. After all, you can't have a society without cities."[1]

Of course, Rendell is right. The only societies without cities are pastoral or nomadic—Sioux Indians and Kalahari bushmen. Otherwise, towns and cities have always played a central role in the development of human civilization. Without cities, epoch-making events such as the Renaissance and the Industrial Revolution could not have occurred, for ideas develop best, and fastest, when large numbers of people congregate in one spot. This remains true even in an age of online social networking.

The history of the United States has been bound up with cities. Although the first British settlement on the Atlantic seaboard, Jamestown, was "modest in scale and primitive in character," as John Reps put it, later communities while still small were distinctly urban.[2] New Haven, Williamsburg, and Savannah were never villages; they were towns—albeit tiny—from the start. Another unusual aspect of towns in the New World was their ambition. Colonial Philadelphia was to be the size of contemporary London, which was then the largest city in Europe. L'Enfant's plan for Washington, D.C., was equally vast. The 1811 Commissioners' Plan for the future expansion of New York City laid out a grid of streets and avenues that was more than seven miles long. All three plans took the best part of a century to realize, but the expectation of growth was there from the beginning. Years later, as Los Angeles grew into a major city, it also took an expansive shape. Instead of a grid, however, its sprawling layout followed the meandering Pacific Electric streetcar lines up and down the coast. The streetcar lines, and later the freeways, produced an urbanism that was unlike anything previously imagined.

American cities continue to surprise. At the beginning of the twentieth century, the five largest cities in the United States were New York, Chicago, Philadelphia, Saint Louis, and Boston. A hundred years later, Philadelphia, Saint Louis, and Boston are off the list—Philadelphia edged out by Phoenix (which in 1900 had barely five thousand inhabitants), Saint Louis no longer among even the top fifty largest cities, and Boston, despite its vaunted comeback, dropping to twenty-third place. Los Angeles, on the other hand, has risen from twenty-eighth to second place, and Houston, which in 1900 was smaller than Fort Wayne, Indiana, is now number four. The population declines of older cities such as Philadelphia, Saint Louis, and Boston, coupled with the unrelenting growth of suburban areas, might suggest that Americans no longer want to live in cities, that we have become, in the words of a recent book title, a "suburban nation."[3] A happy suburban nation, according to a 2008 Pew Research Center national poll. Pew asked Americans if they liked where they lived and found the level of satisfaction among suburbanites (54 percent) to be considerably higher than among city dwellers (44 percent).[4] But while more Americans are happily living in suburbs than ever before, more are living in cities, too. In 1900, a time often described as the heyday of the American city, the United States had only 38 cities with populations larger than one hundred thousand people, and these cities accounted for 14 percent of the total population. By 2006, no less than 258 cities had populations larger than one hundred thousand, and accounted for an impressive 27 percent of the population. This increase was not just a question of the country's growing larger. Over the last twenty-five years, the increase in the proportion of the population living in cities larger than one hundred thousand is almost twice as great as the increase in the population as a whole during the same period.[5]

The question is not whether we want to live in cities. Obviously, a growing number of us do—otherwise we would not build so many of them. The real question is in what *kind* of cities do we want to live? Compact or spread out? Old or new? Big or small?

The answers to these questions are complicated by a blurring of the traditional definition of exactly what constitutes a "city." Not so long ago, big cities were easily distinguished from small towns and rural areas by their quality of life; there were city slickers and country bumpkins, with all the differences that those old stereotypes convey. Today, the nature of suburbs and exurbs makes it difficult to define exactly where the city stops and the countryside begins. Greenwich, Connecticut, for example, looks like a small town, but it's really an extension of Manhattan, as are large parts of the lower Hudson Valley and Bucks County, Pennsylvania. The demographic concept of the "metropolitan area," which groups a city, or even several cities, with surrounding suburbs, was supposed to capture this new reality, but it tells only a part of the story. Forty years ago, the late Irving Kristol pointed out that in terms of the quality of people's lives, it no longer much mattered where they lived. "For the overwhelming fact of American life today," he wrote, "whether this life be lived in a central city or a suburb or a small city—or even in those rural areas where something like a third of our population still resides—is that it is *life in an urban civilization* [emphasis in original]."[6] According to Kristol, "Cities are nothing new; the problem of cities are nothing new; but an urban civilization is very new indeed, and the problems of an urban civilization are without precedent in human history."[7] Thus, the question is, what kind of cities does an urban civilization want?

Judging from the direction that American urbanism has taken during the second half of the twentieth century, one answer of the marketplace is unequivocal—Americans want to live in cities that are spread out. Decentralization and dispersal, the results of a demand for private property, privacy, and detached family homes, have been facilitated by a succession of transportation and communication technologies: first the railroad and the streetcar, later the automobile and the airplane; lastly the telephone, television, and the Internet. In addition, regional shopping malls, FedEx, UPS, and the Home Shopping Network have helped people to spread out. Even environmental technologies—small sewage-treatment facilities and micro power plants—have allowed people to live in more dispersed communities than in the past.

This is not simply suburbanization. All the cities that have experienced vigorous population growth during the second half of the twentieth century—Houston, Phoenix, Dallas, San Jose, Atlanta—have grown by spreading out. These are horizontal cities, with generally low population densities, typically less than ten people per acre, compared to fifteen to twenty people per acre in the older, vertical cities. Horizontal cities depend on automobiles for mass transportation, and on trucks for the movement of goods. In a horizontal city, the difference between city and suburb is indistinct. People in both live chiefly in individual houses rather than in flats or apartment buildings, and the houses are organized in dispersed, semiautonomous planned communities that are different from the urban neighborhoods of the past. Versions of the dispersed city can be found in large cities such as Los Angeles, small cities such as Las Vegas, and in the metropolitan areas surrounding all cities, old and new.

The Technological Reshaping of Metropolitan America, a 1995 report of the federal Office of Technology Assessment, concluded, "Given the technological and economic trends toward decentralization, America's central and inner cities are unlikely to regain their earlier dominance."[8] Decentralization suits an economy that depends on flexibility, adaptability, and rapid change. Dispersal also suits an increasingly heterogeneous society, which is the exact opposite of what is implied by that misleading term *global village*. Despite living in an urban civilization, Americans are not more alike today; they are more dissimilar, and dispersal accommodates these differences.

Horizontal cities have another characteristic—they tend to be new. During the industrial era, advanced infrastructure, good ports, and large workforces gave established cities a head start. In a postindustrial era, however, being old is no longer an advantage; a new community needs but lay down fiber-optic cables, build a walkable downtown, and entice a Whole Foods and a Target to be competitive. I am always struck, returning from Seattle or Denver to my home in Philadelphia, by the urban contrasts. It is not just a century's worth of accumulated industrial grime compared to unsullied newness, or that so much of Philadelphia's infrastructure—the stone viaducts, the narrow turnpikes, the commuter railroad lines—are relics of the past. In Philadelphia, the new always seems slightly makeshift, shoehorned into an old mold that doesn't quite fit. The past is part of the city's charm—and what keeps me here—but it exacts a price in terms of efficiency, convenience, and endless maintenance. An old city is like an old car: it still runs, it will get you there, but it doesn't have the safety features, conveniences, and efficiencies of a newer model.

Creating an urban infrastructure from scratch has many benefits. The Las Vegas–Clark County Library District, for example, which serves 1.5 million residents, does so efficiently with only twelve branches. The library district is able to put all its resources into exceptionally well-equipped branches because, unlike most older cities, it does not have the burden of supporting a large (and often sparsely attended) downtown library. The Las Vegas–Clark County Library District, which was chosen 2003 Library of the Year by the *Library Journal,* is also effective because it is not a city department but an independent institution, with its own payroll, financial management, and even its own taxing authority. This financial autonomy is important, as shown recently in Philadelphia, where the city government, facing a fiscal crisis, threatened a "doomsday budget" that would have required laying off three thousand municipal employees and closing all the public libraries.

Newness has other advantages. New cities generally have new, and often streamlined, building regulations, new social compacts between management and labor, and new ways of doing things. Houston's absence of zoning, its less restrictive building regulations, and its lower construction costs, for example, mean that, according to the 2006 census, the average owner-occupied dwelling cost $126,000, compared to $496,000 in New York City.[9] Since incomes in greater Houston are only slightly lower than in New York, that makes the city much more affordable for the middle class and, according to Harvard economist Edward L. Glaeser, accounts for Houston's greater appeal; between 2000 and 2007, the city grew by 19.4 percent, compared to just 2.7 percent for New York.[10] The presence of a large middle-class workforce also explains why

Houston has more blue-collar manufacturing jobs than New York.

Another answer to what kind of cities we want seems to be "warmer." A 2008 national survey of the major metropolitan areas that appealed most to people found that the favorites — Denver, San Diego, Seattle, Orlando, and Tampa — all shared "warm weather, a casual lifestyle and rapid growth."[11] In fact, all of the top ten cities on the list were in temperate climates, seven in the West and three in the South. It also helps if a city is close to attractive natural amenities such as lakes, mountains, beaches, or the desert. Given the popular interest in the outdoors, and outdoor activities, nearby wilderness areas have become important urban amenities. As David Brooks put it, "These [favorite cities] are places where you can imagine yourself with a stuffed garage — filled with skis, kayaks, soccer equipment, hiking boots and boating equipment. These are places you can imagine yourself leading an active outdoor lifestyle."[12] Industrial cities didn't need beautiful settings; postindustrial cities do.

Virtually every technological innovation of the last fifty years has facilitated, if not actually encouraged, urban dispersal. But the long-term effects of new technologies are often unpredictable. The telephone is, on the face of it, a decentralizing device. Yet telephone communication made working in high-rise office buildings practicable, which in turn produced the concentrated central business district. When people started commuting in cars, an unexpected fallout was the death of the evening newspaper, which used to be read on the streetcar trip home. People couldn't read in their cars, but they could listen to the radio, and that moribund medium found new life. Who could have foreseen that the combination of car radios and cellular phones would give rise to a new format, talk radio, and a new and potent political force, the talk-radio host? Laptops, personal digital assistants, and cell phones are held to be the tips of a great dispersal iceberg, but the migration of work to the motel room and the home office has been accompanied by a countervailing trend: the need for face-to-face contact. That is why there are more conferences, retreats, and conventions than ever before. That is also why so many industries—finance, publishing, entertainment, high tech, and communications—cluster together geographically.

Thus, even as dispersal appears to be the order of the day, concentration is making a comeback. Sometimes concentration takes new forms: power centers, office parks, theme parks, and villagelike planned communities in the middle of nowhere. Sometimes the results of concentration are more familiar: downtown entertainment districts, historic neighborhoods, waterfront esplanades, and urban parks. All such gathering places are evidence of the age-old desire for human contact, crowds, variety, and expanded individual choices. This desire has breathed new life into many small cities, especially college towns, which, with their attendant research facilities, office parks, university hospitals, and cultural amenities, have blossomed and are among the fastest-growing and most attractive places to live and work.[13] Part of this blossoming is the result of technology. Cable television, regional airlines, catalog shopping, and the Internet have brought big-city conveniences to small cities. But when college towns succeed as attractive and vital places to live—and by no

Wilderness areas as urban amenities:
the Wenatchee Mountains and Wenatchee, Washington.

means all do—the result is a potent synergy between higher education, information-age industries, and people's preferences for smaller, more intimate communities.*

The appeal of the college town as a place to live and work is part of a larger trend that Kristol identified as early as 1970. "If we are a 'nation of cities,'" he wrote, "we are also becoming to an ever greater degree a nation of relatively small and middle-sized cities."[14] That was true then and it is even truer today. In 1970, slightly more Americans lived in small (between 25,000 and 250,000 inhabitants) cities than in big (larger than 250,000)

---

*Scale is critical. Large universities, as Jane Jacobs observed, are self-sufficient, single-function entities that disrupt the small-scale heterogeneity of a city. This often has a negative effect, whether it is a large city (West Philadelphia and the University of Pennsylvania) or a small one (New Haven and Yale).

The attractions of the small city in Santa Fe, New Mexico.

cities, reversing the situation of a decade earlier, when big cities dominated, as they had done for years. By 2006, although the total urban population had increased, the gap had considerably widened, and more than half again as many people lived in small cities as in large. Indeed, since 1970 the proportion of the urban population living in large cities has steadily declined, while the percentage living in small cities has grown, suggesting that what Americans *don't* want is to live in large metropolitan areas.[15] This was confirmed by a 2008 Pew poll, which found "not a single one of the 30 [largest] metropolitan areas was judged by a majority of respondents as a place where they'd like to live."[16]

Thus, for many Americans, the answer to "What kind of cities do we want?" seems to be not just dispersed, new, and warmer, but also smaller. In some cases, much smaller. In 2007, the fastest appreciating residential real estate values in the nation were not in San Francisco, Boston, and New York City, but in Corvallis, Oregon (population 53,000); Grand Junction, Colorado (population 46,000); and Wenatchee, Washington (population 28,000).[17] These small cities are examples of what Joel Garreau has christened the Santa Fe effect, referring to the New Mexico city that, while small (population 62,000), has a variety of big-city amenities including many restaurants and shops, an opera company, a chamber-music festival, and a renowned film festival. Places such as Wenatchee, a hundred miles from Seattle at the eastern foot of the Cascade Mountains, are characterized by attractive natural surroundings (deserts, lakes, mountains, rivers), moderate climates, and a degree of urbanity that belies their small size and their often remote location. "The core premise of the Santa-Feing hypothesis is that the same kind of choice is now available to millions of Americans," writes Joel Garreau. "Today, people of means are attracted by this scenario of dramatically different settlement patterns that feature new aggregation—dispersed."[18]

In a recent international ranking of global cities, New York had a preeminent position, and Los Angeles, Chicago, and Washington, D.C., were highly rated in categories such as business, human capital, and information exchange.[19] All are large cities, a reminder that although small and medium-size cities are outstripping big cities in the American public's favor, big cities still have a role to play. They are breeding grounds for budding entrepreneurs, for example, and start-up businesses continue to fuel the economies of New York, Los Angeles, and Houston. Big cities are not just large concentrations of people, they are also concentrations of knowledge, skills, and information. That is why the largest employers in many big cities are universities, hospitals, and medical research facilities. As Glaeser puts it, "Spatial proximity may no longer be important for the delivery of widgets, but it is vital for the transfer of ideas."[20]

People come together in big cities for specific reasons. Some of these reasons are the same as they've always been; some are different. People come to work—not to sew clothing or to build locomotives, as they did in the past, but to do brain-work. Big cities with well-educated workforces (Seattle, Boston, San Francisco) continue to be the best places for financial and communications work, as well as for creative enterprises. People also visit big cities to play, to spend time in a casino, tour a museum, go to an IMAX theater, to rub shoulders with their fellows—to simply be part of a crowd. Whether working or playing, people want safety and convenience. They want cities with good policing, transportation, and sanitation. They also want downtowns that are lively—the Jane Jacobs imperative.

Developers have learned that urban vitality is the product not only of commercial and retail activities, but also of residents. That explains the success of mixed-use downtown developments such as Battery Park City, which respond to a relatively new phenomenon: people want to live downtown. This desire is more complicated than the media, which regularly trumpet the "revival" of this or that downtown, suggest. A recent study of forty-four downtowns found that the residential populations of different downtowns vary considerably.[21] Some downtowns are home to a lot of people, some to few; some downtowns are dense, others are sparsely occupied; and some are growing, while others are stagnating. The guarded conclusion of the study is that following two decades during which the number of downtown residents declined—sometimes precipitously—these populations in some cities appear to be modestly growing. The detailed picture is uneven, however. Between 1970 and 1990, a period of slow economic growth, most downtowns lost population, although the downtown residential populations of a few cities (Cincinnati, Pittsburgh, and Portland, Oregon) continued to grow. During the booming 1990s, some downtowns—Baltimore, Milwaukee, Saint Louis, and Detroit—showed little sign of revival, but several (Boston, Philadelphia, Atlanta, Dallas, Cleveland, Phoenix, and Denver) recaptured some—though not all—of their earlier loss. Downtown Houston, which actually gained population between 1970 and 1990, lost some during the following decade. Most downtowns have grown less quickly than their suburbs, but the growth of seven—Chicago, Cleveland, Los Angeles, New York, Norfolk, San Francisco, and Seattle—has outstripped that of their surrounding metropolitan area.

Clearly, downtowns are not created equal. To be viable, a downtown requires a critical mass; it takes a certain number of people to support a variety of supermarkets, hardware stores, bakeries, bars, and restaurants. Ten thousand inhabitants is often cited as the minimum population for a viable neighborhood, but a successful downtown must be much larger than that, sufficiently large to be a magnet for the surrounding city and the region. Probably a downtown residential population closer to fifty thousand is the minimum required to achieve a truly urban way of life. Only six American downtowns currently have this critical mass: New York City (which has Midtown and Downtown), Boston, Philadelphia, Chicago, and San Francisco. Los Angeles is close, so is Washington, D.C., but such highly touted examples of downtown revival as Seattle and Portland, Oregon, are well below the line; so are Cleveland and Pittsburgh. Downtown Dallas, which experienced rapid growth during the last decade, will take another fifty years at the present rate to reach forty thousand; Denver, which is often cited as another model of downtown revival, will need almost twice as long.

In addition to a minimum critical mass, a successful downtown also needs density; it's no good having a lot of people if they are spread out. The gross population density of Midtown Manhattan, for example, is more than eighty people per acre, which is unusually high for an American city. Downtowns such as San Francisco, Boston, and Philadelphia have gross densities in the neighborhood of twenty people per acre, which probably represents the threshold necessary to support an active street life as well as viable mass transit, which are both requirements for successful downtown living. However, when the population density of a downtown drops to suburban levels (below ten people per acre), people are living too far apart—or there are too few of them relative to the area—to create the requisite urban atmosphere or to support an urban infrastructure. Atlanta and Dallas have relatively large downtown populations, but their densities remain extremely low. Phoenix and Houston, with small downtown populations and low densities, likewise have a long way to go.

Downtowns can't be spread out. They are typically about four square miles in area; that is, the edge is about a twenty-minute walk from the center. Walkability is important since it is one of the competitive advantages that downtowns offer compared to suburbs. However, the concentration of a downtown also produces high land prices, which together with labor costs, congestion, government bureaucracy, and taxes increases the cost of downtown housing. As a result, most lively and attractive downtowns have become wealthy enclaves—of the upwardly mobile and the retired well-to-do.

Downtown living does not contradict the general American preference for small communities. Garreau observes that face-to-face places are not necessarily only small cities but can also be neighborhoods and downtown districts embedded in large cities. Residential neighborhoods such as Chelsea and SoHo in New York, Society Hill in Philadelphia, or Adams Morgan and Georgetown in Washington, D.C., could be described as (very prosperous) small towns located within big cities.

The desire of some Americans to live downtown must be put in perspective, however. In 2000, the forty-four largest downtowns (ranging from Midtown Manhattan, Chicago, and Philadelphia, to tiny Albuquerque and Austin, Texas) were together home to fewer than 1 million people.[22] In other words, the number of Americans who actually live downtown is only *0.3 percent* of the entire population. Downtown residents are also untypical of the population at large; according to a recent study, 90 percent of people living in downtowns across the country are single, unrelated individuals sharing an apartment or childless couples.[23] "Today, elite cities often attract tourists, upper-class populations working in the highest end of business services, and those who can service their needs, as well as the nomadic young, many of whom later move on to other locales," writes Joel Kotkin. "This increasingly ephemeral city seems to place its highest values on such transient values as hipness, coolness, artfulness, and fashionability."[24]

Some people want to be fashionable, some people don't want to live in cities at all. There isn't a single answer to the question "What kind of cities do we want?" because different people want so many different things. While the majority of us appear to prefer dispersed small cities, a significant minority want to live in concentrated big cities, and a tiny fraction is prepared to pay the price of living in the very center of things. Most of us want lively downtowns, at least to visit if not to live in. Nor is it simply a question of individual preferences; we want different things at different times: an exciting big city when we are young, beginning a career, and looking for a mate; a dispersed small city close to nature when we are raising a family; a culture-rich downtown when we are empty nesters; and a walkable small city in a warm climate when we retire. If cities are shaped by popular demand, one can expect them to exhibit a variety that is no less rich and diverse than the variety of Americans themselves.

11

The Kind of Cities We Need

Urban growth is not driven only by people's demands—what we want—it is also influenced by involuntary needs. The dense, walled European towns of the Middle Ages, for example, were the result of their inhabitants' need to seek common safety behind protective walls, not of a desire for a compact way of life. American settlers located towns near safe anchorages because they depended on water transport, not because they wanted a marine view. The unprecedented growth of industrial cities in the nineteenth century, which so dismayed Ebenezer Howard, was produced by the need for large pools of labor of the urban factories that had replaced rural farms as the chief source of employment.

Transportation remains one of the most important external forces that influence the shape of cities. In the preindustrial world, the size and density of cities was determined by the relatively short distance that people could travel on foot from their homes to their workplaces; for the wealthy, who could afford horses and carriages, this distance was somewhat greater. Starting in the nineteenth century, horse-drawn omnibuses, electric trolleys, railroads, and subways enabled cities to spread out and encouraged the growth of residential suburbs at the periphery. In the twentieth century, automobiles doubled and tripled commuting distances, allowing far-out exurban development to flourish. Air travel, too, influenced urbanization by making relatively remote cities more accessible.

Transportation accounts for more than two-thirds of American oil consumption. The average global price of crude oil during the post–Second World War period was $27 a barrel (in 2008 dollars). After a low of $16 at the beginning of 1999, the price rose to $50 in 2005, and passed $145 in the summer of 2008. The chief reasons for the price increase were greater demand caused by China's and India's industrial booms, uncertainty about future supplies, and the inability—or unwillingness—of suppliers and governments to increase production. Oil prices were further increased to American consumers since crude oil was priced in U.S. dollars, and in 2008 the dollar was weak compared to other major currencies. Oil prices have spiked before—in the 1970s, when the Organization of Petroleum Exporting Countries imposed an embargo following the Arab-Israeli war, and in the 1980s, during the Iran-Iraq war. The spike of 2008 did not last long, and prices have since fallen, but the immediate impact on the economy—and on people's behavior—offers a revealing portent of things to come. Sooner or later, we will be paying more for gas again.

At first glance, higher energy prices should benefit cities, especially cities with mass transit, since with higher oil prices the cost of traveling by bus or subway increases much more slowly than the cost of operating a private automobile. The 2008 gas-price spike, for example, produced an instant change as mass-transit ridership rates rose 5 to 15 percent, not only in traditionally transit-oriented cities such as New York, Chicago, and Boston, but also in cities with new transit systems, such as San Francisco, Denver, Minneapolis, Seattle, and Dallas–Fort Worth. Bus and train lines in Houston, Nashville, Salt Lake City, and Charlotte, North Carolina, also experienced increases.[1] Cities have several transportation advantages. Since they are more compact than suburbs, walking and bicycling are feasible, as is using scooters or micro-cars. Higher population densities enable large cities to offer a greater variety of stores, services, and cultural amenities within relatively small areas, further minimizing local travel. Lastly, urban housing, especially in the centers of older cities, tends to be smaller, more compact, and more closely packed—row houses, walk-up flats, and apartment buildings—and hence produces lower heating and air-conditioning loads than large, freestanding suburban houses.

High gas prices also represent an opportunity for cities to increase their share of employment, since for the first time in a long time, size and density would be competitive advantages. But a major snag is that most cities do not currently have a wide range of employment opportunities. The high-tech jobs in the San Francisco region, for example, tend to be suburban; the same is true in Seattle and Boston. Moreover, for corporate employers, large cities currently have a number of significant disincentives: faltering school systems, high tax burdens, unwieldy municipal bureaucracies, poor services, and unresponsive governments.

For one group, job opportunities are not an issue: retirees. While downtown multifamily housing has traditionally targeted high-income empty nesters, more demand for downtown living may now come from middle-income, aging suburban home-owners who are nervous about rising gas and heating-oil prices. While the majority of lifelong suburbanites are unlikely to suddenly become urbanites, some suburbanites on fixed incomes would see city living as a hedge against rising prices.

Higher energy costs also produce negative effects on cities. Part of the downtown housing boom of the last two decades was fueled by so-called reverse commuters, people whose jobs were in the suburbs but who lived in the city. Reverse commuting has been the fastest growing segment of all commuting trips, especially in large cites, although suburb-to-suburb commuting still constitutes the majority of all commuting trips.[2] The easiest way for reverse commuters to save money is to move closer to their jobs—that is, back to the suburbs. (Some evidence suggests that this occurred in 1981, the last time gas prices spiked.)

Rising prices for gas, as well as for other energy-related sectors (home heating, food, services), would likely lead to reductions in discretionary spending on recreation and tourism, which are both economic mainstays of large cities. A reduction in the number of tourists, museum visitors, and theatergoers would hit cities hard. Higher travel costs would first affect tourist cities such as Orlando, Miami, Las Vegas, and San Francisco, which depend on distant visitors. Cutbacks on less profitable schedules by struggling airlines are already reducing service to smaller cities, which will affect their rates of growth. Lastly, rising air travel costs will reduce nonessential business travel, such as annual meetings and conventions, both key urban industries. So, whatever advantages accrue to cities as a result of new residents, these are likely to be offset by losses in short-term visitors.

It is too soon to judge the effect of the current recession on cities, but it is likely to have effects similar to those of high gas prices. Cities are already feeling the pinch of less leisure and business travel, for example, with a resulting drop-off in hotel bookings and restaurant business. Residential construction has halted in cities as well as suburbs, and the downtown real estate boom that many cities experienced in the last two decades has halted with it. Shrinking tax bases are putting a severe strain on municipal services, and with reduced services downtowns are less attractive places to live. During the current recession, the downtown populations of many cities will likely shrink, as they did during the slowdown of 1970–90.

Higher oil prices would obviously affect suburbs and dispersed cities, which depend on automobiles. Over time, suburban drivers could be expected to make more use of car pools, and mass transit where that is available, with a demand for more bus routes, at least in denser suburbs. Transit-oriented communities would have an advantage, and densities would rise in suburban town centers. Since suburbs are built to relatively low densities, even modest densification would go a long way to reduce car dependency, at least for local trips. However, the main change will likely be behavioral. When oil hit $60 a barrel, personal expenditures on gasoline actually fell slightly in real terms, showing how quickly consumers could change their driving habits and substitute smaller for larger cars (in the first half of 2008, sales of large pickup trucks and sport utility vehicles dropped 25 and 30 percent respectively).[3] Even when gas prices are no longer high, this preference may continue. According to the Department of Transportation, the top ten vehicles purchased under the federal Cash for Clunkers program, which encouraged owners to trade in old cars for more fuel-efficient models, were all subcompacts, compacts, and mini-SUVs.[4]

One would expect the demand for denser, walkable suburban communities to increase. This would help not only new developments but also older, inner suburbs, which tend to be more compact. Older suburbs, which have seen deterioration of their housing stock and lower real estate values, might attract new residents as higher gas prices cause home buyers to consider commuting time, access to mass transit, density, and closeness to urban centers. The new exurbs that have recently sprung up at the far edges of metropolitan areas may fare less well. Exurban home buyers trade long commuting times for cheaper housing, and when long commutes become more expensive, the trade-off will be less attractive.

Since the majority of Americans now live and work in the suburbs, the market would likely adjust to high gas prices not only by moving additional jobs and retail closer to suburban residents, but also by developing more efficient heating and air-conditioning systems and, of course, producing smaller, more energy-efficient cars, as well as vehicles that run on alternative fuels such as ethanol blends and natural gas. So far, only one manufacturer produces a natural-gas vehicle, and filling stations are rare, but in many ways natural gas represents the simplest technological alternative. All-electric cars still await improvements in battery technology; in the meantime electric-gas hybrids are an option. In mid-2008, Toyota announced that it sold more than 1 million Prius hybrids, and Honda has just unveiled its own model. Honda also recently introduced a hydrogen fuel-cell car, the FCX Clarity, which is said to be twice as energy efficient as a gas-electric hybrid, and three times more than a standard gasoline-powered car. While the FCX remains prohibitively expensive, the promise of alternative transportation is real. If automobile manufacturers can produce an affordable car that does not require gasoline—or uses considerably less—the suburbs would get a new lease on life.

Natural-gas vehicles significantly reduce environmentally harmful carbon monoxide emissions and also cut down on emissions of various oxides of nitrogen and reactive hydrocarbons. Hydrogen fuel-cell cars emit only water and none of the gases believed to induce global warning. Electric vehicles produce no emissions at all (although electricity generated by fuel-powered power plants does). So, if there is a silver lining to the high-oil-price cloud, it is that most energy-conserving or energy-substituting strategies—such as driving smaller and more fuel-efficient cars, driving less, using alternative transportation and mass transit, densifying neighborhoods, and building more energy-efficient houses—also improve the global environment.

In 1950, global emissions of carbon dioxide amounted to 6 billion tons a year. Thanks to population growth, urbanization, the expansion of wealth, and massive industrialization around the world, by 2008 emissions increased fivefold to 30 billion tons a year. If nothing is done to reduce emissions, by 2058 they will be 60 billion tons a year. Thus, to control global warning, whose effects are already beginning to be felt, it will be necessary to take drastic measures just to stay at the present level of emissions, never mind actually making real reductions. For example, to reduce the number of coal-fired generating plants, nuclear capacity in the United States will have to be doubled.

To reduce car emissions, Americans will either have to drive half as many miles per year, or cars will have to be twice as efficient (although some evidence suggests that owning more efficient cars actually increases the amount that people drive).

Buildings use a lot of energy. The construction and operation of residential and commercial buildings consume as much as 40 percent of the energy used in the United States today, so reducing global emissions requires changing the way that buildings are designed and built. So-called green buildings incorporate a variety of devices and techniques. Energy consumption is reduced by using highly transparent glass, which decreases artificial illumination and reduces heat loads due to electric lights. Coatings on glass, or shading devices, prevent heat-causing solar radiation from entering buildings. In office buildings, lighting systems automatically adjust to complement the varying levels of natural light in different parts of a space to reduce the need for artificial illumination. Conditioned air is distributed through the floor rather than from the ceiling (as in most buildings), which means that since it travels a shorter distance it can be cooled less—and pressurized less— saving energy and increasing comfort. In residential buildings, openable windows permit natural ventilation to take advantage of wind currents and convection to cool spaces. Rainwater is collected and used for cooling systems, and for landscape irrigation. Roofs are light-colored to reflect heat. Building materials are chosen not only to fulfill their immediate function, but also on the basis of energy consumed in production, transportation distances, ease of maintenance, and potential for eventual reuse.

These technological fixes are undoubtedly useful, but they

conceal a basic truth. Rather than trying to change behavior to reduce carbon emissions, politicians and entrepreneurs have sold greening to the public as a kind of accessorizing. "Keep doing what you're doing," is the message, just add a solar panel, a wind turbine, a bamboo floor, whatever. But a solar-heated house in the suburbs is still a house in the suburbs, and if you have to drive to it—even in a Prius—it's hardly green. "The average New Yorker," writes David Owen in *Green Metropolis*, "annually generates 7.1 metric tons of greenhouse gases, a lower rate than that of residents of any other American city, and less than 30 percent of the national average, which is 24.5 metric tons; Manhattanites generate even less."[5] He argues that what really makes a city green are not grassy roofs and rainwater cisterns, but density. In a suburban office campus, for example, people work in low, sprawling buildings and drive between them; in a city, people work in compact multistory buildings, use elevators (which are inherently energy efficient since they are counterweighted), and walk to lunch. Owen suggests that rather than conceiving of Utopian solutions, or complicated technological add-ons, planners should study existing cities that already offer "instructive examples of how to achieve low-impact urban living," citing Manhattan and Hong Kong.[6]

Although extremely dense vertical cities conserve more energy and resources, they are not really models; simply put, the demand for Manhattan-type living is limited. But if Americans are to significantly reduce their carbon footprints, they will have to consider densification. Per capita carbon dioxide emissions in American cities are estimated to be twice as high as in Europe, and the so-called ecological footprints of American cities—the land area beyond the city proper that

is required for food production, energy and resources supply, and waste assimilation—are correspondingly large.[7] "The
low-density auto-dependent American landscape makes sustainable living—such as walking, bicycling, or public transport—difficult," writes Timothy Beatley, an urban-planning
professor at the University of Virginia and the author of *Green
Urbanism*. "American cities consequently have high carbon
dioxide emissions, produce large amounts of waste, and draw
in large amounts of energy and resources."[8]

It will be difficult for Americans to emulate European cities, with their dense historic centers, different housing patterns,
lower reliance on automobiles, and highly regulated urban
development. Is there another model? The new Israeli city of
Modi'in provides some useful lessons for achieving a denser
and greener—in both senses—urbanism. Located halfway
between Jerusalem and Tel Aviv, Modi'in has been built from
scratch on open land that was previously a military reservation.
Planning started in 1989, the first residents moved in 1993, and
today the population has reached eighty thousand. The planning team is led by Moshe Safdie, who gained renown as the
designer of Habitat 67, an innovative housing complex that was
an example of what he called a three-dimensional community.
Of Habitat he wrote, "I wanted to demonstrate that a city could
be built at a population density comparable with the downtown
areas of Montreal or Boston without compromising the quality of environment of each particular urban activity, whether
it was shopping, or housing, or work."[9] Habitat, an attempt to
raise housing density through a radically different design, was
basically a megastructure solution. Modi'in is different: a city
informed by post–Jane Jacobs urban design. I asked Safdie how

Jacobs had influenced his thinking. "No doubt Jacobs's book had a great impact," he answered. "At the time we were all struggling with Miesian planning and the urban-renewal syndrome, and it's interesting how the responses to Jane Jacobs differed. On one hand, the New Urbanism setting the clock back; in my case, actually feeling we needed to deal with her observations and values looking forward to a denser, more urban environment." Modi'in includes a mix of housing types: apartments in tall buildings (located on hilltops to serve as landmarks); closely spaced single-family row houses; and the majority (two-thirds) consisting of walk-up flats in small three- and four-story buildings, six to eight units per building.

Safdie describes Modi'in as a conscious attempt to create a "normal" as opposed to a "planned" city. "The difference concerns a clearer articulation between the public domain and individual buildings," he says. "In normal cities, buildings are organized along public streets. There is a variety of building types resulting from construction over time by many architects and developers, thus enhancing the identity of individual buildings. Planned cities with large-scale projects, in contrast, are large compounds within which many buildings are clustered without a street address. At Modi'in we were determined to achieve a finer-grain organization and parcelization of land, with a greater variety in the design of individual buildings." To achieve this variety, Safdie's team adopted a novel method of planning that combined overall guiding principles with piecemeal development. A master plan established the main thoroughfares, the general outlines of the neighborhoods, and the location of the town center. However, the detailed urban design of individual neighborhoods was del-

The new city of Modi'in is a model for urban densification.

egated to several independent teams of architects and planners who were required to follow urban-design guidelines. (Safdie's office planned one of the residential neighborhoods, as well as the town center.) The decentralization continued at the level of buildings, since within the neighborhoods, housing sites were allocated to different private developers (as in Battery Park City). Since the developers worked with a variety of architects, and since the neighborhood planners interpreted Safdie's urban guidelines with varying degrees of strictness, the result is much more heterogeneous than most planned communities, more like a normal city.

What sets Modi'in apart from strictly market-based planned communities is the emphasis on public uses. The residential neighborhoods, for example, are located on the hilly slopes, but the valley floors are reserved for parks, parkways, and sites for kindergartens, schools, clinics, and small shopping centers. The

Modern housing along a traditional street.

city is planned to be drivable, but much of the housing is within walking distance of the valley facilities, which are reached by means of landscaped walks that descend the hillsides and recall the pedestrian stairs of San Francisco and Montmartre. The low and dense town center, consisting of five- and six-story buildings, includes a mixture of offices, civic uses, and apartment buildings. An indoor shopping mall resembles a bazaar and contains a community theater as well as an adjacent outdoor market. Perhaps the most remarkable feature of the town center is the absence of surface parking lots and parking garages—all the parking is underground.

Although Modi'in is not specifically designed to be green, it contains many resource- and energy-saving strategies. Density facilitates walkability as well as a local bus system. While

The town center, which is a cross between a shopping mall
and a bazaar, includes an outdoor market
and a community theater.

the inhabitants, like most Israelis, own cars, there is a train to
Tel Aviv (a twenty-minute ride), and a second line is under construction to Jerusalem. The forested areas of the hilly and otherwise barren site are kept in their natural states, and a wide
greenbelt surrounds the city. Adding in nature preserves, protected archaeological sites, and open sports and recreation
zones leaves almost a third of the eight-thousand-acre site
unbuilt. The landscaping of parks is designed to minimize irrigation, with drought-resistant plantings and few lawns. Storm
water is retained on the site and used for irrigation or infil-
trated into an aquifer. Following national standards, all household sewage and gray water is piped to a regional recycling and
purification plant, from whence treated water is distributed to

agricultural areas. Through such measures, Israel recycles as much as 75 percent of its water, a remarkable figure. It has been estimated that 90 percent of homes in Israel use a solar water heater, which is required by law, and every dwelling in Modi'in has a solar heater on the roof.

Walking around Modi'in, I can't shake the feeling of being in an early-twentieth-century Garden City, albeit hilly and with palm trees. This feeling is heightened by the appearance of the housing, which is mostly in the practical, modern style that is common throughout Israel, although one neighborhood, with tiled roofs and bright colors, reminds me of Southern California. Overall, the simple, white buildings recall the International Style common in older parts of Tel Aviv. The planners of Modi'in long debated whether it should be a "white city" like Tel Aviv (where buildings are plastered and painted white), or a "stone city" like Jerusalem (where so-called Jerusalem limestone is required on the exteriors of buildings). They decided on a combination of the two: stone in the town center and the valley buildings, but elsewhere, either plaster or stone.

When talking about the design of Modi'in, Safdie frequently refers to Patrick Geddes's original plan for Tel Aviv. In the 1920s, during the British Mandate in Palestine, Geddes, who had earlier laid out neighborhoods in Jerusalem, was commissioned to create a master plan for the new city of Tel Aviv, which had been founded by Jewish settlers in 1906. He laid out the core of the city according to Garden City principles, with parks, boulevards, and landscaped pedestrian walkways. The result is both urban and gardenlike. During the 1930s, émigré German architects such as Richard Kauffman and the great Erich Mendelsohn built *Gartenstädte* neighborhoods in Tel Aviv and Jerusalem. Despite Jane Jacobs's criticism of the Garden City in *The Death and Life of Great American Cities*, these neighborhoods have flourished and are much prized and admired today as humane and attractive living environments.

Tel Aviv incorporated two vital principles of Geddes's vision. The first, as Mumford, who considered Geddes "my master," explained, was to plan cities at a human scale to avoid the sprawling modern megalopolis, which Mumford called "the last word in imageless urban amorphousness."[10] The second was to avoid high densities, since "housing designed at three hundred to four hundred people to the acre—to say nothing of the greater number some favor—is not conducive to health, neighborly cooperation, or adequate child care," Mumford argued.[11] In Modi'in, which has a population density of about fifty people per acre and is intended to grow to a quarter of a million people, Safdie and his team have shown that Geddes's and Mumford's ideas still have relevance.*

Modi'in demonstrates that green urbanism does not require newfangled technological devices, but something more old-fashioned: good planning. Adapting these lessons to American conditions will require ingenuity. While densities of fifty people per acre are not uncommon in Israel, where most people live in apartments and flats, the majority of Americans live in single-family houses, at densities of ten to fifteen people per

---

*Curiously, fifty people per acre is about the same as Raymond Unwin's "twelve houses to the acre," given the larger household sizes of his time. It is also similar to the density of midrise cities such as today's Copenhagen and Stockholm.

acre. Yet efforts will have to be made to achieve a denser way of life, while at the same time taking into account people's desire for dispersed living in smaller cities. Broadacre will have to become Narrowacre. Densification does not necessarily mean high-rise apartments; it can be achieved through a combination of infill developments in cities and towns, and smaller lots and more compact (and probably somewhat smaller) houses in the suburbs. It will also require a greater variety of housing choices, not only freestanding houses on large lots, but twins and row houses, housing terraces, walk-up apartments, clusters of cottages, bungalow courts, and compact mews—all time-tested models that are worth revisiting.

Low-density communities can afford to ignore the public realm, but increasing the density of housing will require paying more attention to public amenities such as well-designed streets, public spaces, and town centers. The creative use of open green space in Modi'in, like the combination of development and parkland in Brooklyn Bridge Park, shows how active landscapes can complement dense living. Not Le Corbusier's model of buildings-in-a-park but buildings *and* parks. A Garden City approach might be a useful compromise between dense urbanism and spread-out suburbanism. Forest Hills Gardens, for example, is a hundred years old but still has lessons to teach. With its mixture of low-rise apartments and different types of single-family houses, it reaches a gross density of about thirty-five people per acre—a good starting point. A more radical, and more urban, solution is the Yards in Washington, D.C. With its combination of old and new structures, residential and commercial uses, and social and market housing, it shows that it is possible to achieve high density without tall buildings.

The Yards is being completed, but many new urban developments remain on the drawing boards since the present recession has produced a virtual halt in construction and urban development. The last time this happened for an extended period was during the Great Depression of the 1930s, a building interruption that extended through the end of the Second World War. The effect on architecture and city building was devastating, and not just because little was built. The disruption was not only physical but intellectual: offices closed, careers were cut short, practitioners took early retirement, and the continuity of practice was interrupted. Much professional knowledge, normally transmitted between generations through apprenticeship, was lost. The urban accomplishments of the early 1900s, such as Forest Hills Gardens, depended on teamwork—among developers, planners, architects, landscape architects, builders, and public administrators—and the lack of new projects allowed these networks to unravel. Thus, by the 1950s, when the economy revived and cities began to think of rebuilding and replanning, few seasoned professionals were available. At the same time, a widely held view among the public was that the times called for change. This explains the willingness to attempt radical and untested urban interventions such as urban renewal, traffic separation, high-rise social housing in the cities, and dispersed planned communities in the suburbs.

The current stalled economy has produced a call for massive government spending in the public sector. Inevitably, much of this spending will take place in cities and metropolitan areas. Architects and planners will once again be tempted to implement grand urban visions—twenty-first-century versions of urban renewal and the Radiant City. The temptation will be particularly great since government-funded projects provide freedom from the constraints imposed by the market, an opportunity to replace demand-side urbanism with supply-side planning; us telling them what they should like, just as in the good old days. This temptation must be resisted. The urban lessons of the last hundred years should not go unheeded. Small is not always beautiful, but piecemeal urbanism has a long and proven track record. Effective planning should recognize that while the market is not always right, an aggregation of individual decisions is generally closer to the mark than the plans of willful urban visionaries, however exciting those plans appear on paper. Nor is striving to replicate the Bilbao Effect the solution to urban revitalization. History does not always have all the answers—new problems do sometimes require new solutions—but it behooves us to keep one eye on the past as we venture into the future. This is not about nostalgia or summoning an imagined past, but freedom from history is no freedom at all. The next city will include much that is new, but to succeed it cannot ignore what came before. Linking the past with the present, and seeing the old anew, has always been part of our improvised urban condition.

Acknowledgments

In January 2007, I aired some of the ideas that appear in this book in a public lecture given at the National Building Museum in Washington, D.C., on the occasion of receiving a prize named in honor of the distinguished architectural historian Vincent Scully. I want to thank both Scully, whose writing on architecture and urbanism has been an inspiration over the years, and Chase Rynd, director of the National Building Museum. I returned to the museum in 2008 to deliver the Charles Atherton Memorial Lecture, speaking on the vertical dimension of the city, a subject dear to Washingtonians' hearts since the capital is the last American city to have preserved a building-height limit.

Much of my writing on cities first saw the light of day in the biannual *Wharton Real Estate Review*, which I cofounded with my friend Peter Linneman. I want to acknowledge his insightful advice, as well as the stimulating work of many urban scholars and real estate professionals whose work has appeared in the pages of the review over the last decade, including Jonathan Barnett, Eugenie L. Birch, Robert Bruegmann, David De Long, Anthony Downs, Andres Duany, Douglas Frantz, Charles E. Fraser, Joel Garreau, Edward L. Glaeser, Jacques

ACKNOWLEDGMENTS

N. Gordon, William Grigsby, Joseph Gyourko, Joel Kotkin, John Landis, Robert C. Larson, Anne Vernez Moudon, Randall O'Toole, Georgette Phillips, Harvey Rabinowitz, Albert B. Rattner, William Rawn, Kenneth T. Rosen, Saskia Sassen, Andrejs Skaburskis, Robert A. M. Stern, David Sucher, Anita Summers, Kerry Vandell, and Susan Wachter. Thanks to Joe Gyourko, director of the Zell-Lurie Real Estate Center, for his continued support of the review. My Wharton colleague Robert Inman provided an opportunity to contribute a chapter on urban space to *Making Cities Work: Prospects and Policies for Urban America*, which allowed me to explore the subject of chapter 9. The late Lloyd Rodwin invited me to give a seminar at the department of city planning in MIT (later published in *The Profession of City Planning: Changes, Images and Challenges: 1950–2000*), which helped to clarify my ideas on the declining influence of city planners on the physical form of cities. Thanks also to Nathan Glazer for his recollections of Jane Jacobs.

This is a book about places as well as ideas. My appreciation to Michael Van Valkenburgh and Matt Urbanski, who explained Brooklyn Bridge Park to me; to David Bagnoli, who accompanied me to Reston Town Center; to Deborah Ratner Salzberg, Kirsten A. Brinker, and David R. Smith of Forest City Washington, and Dan McCabe of Urban Atlantic, who provided useful information about the Yards; and to Robert A. M. Stern, whose writing introduced me to Forest Hills Gardens. Alex Cooper and Jaquelin T. Robertson shared their early proposal for Ground Zero. In Israel, my appreciation to my old friend Moshe Safdie for inviting me to visit Modi'in, to Miron Cohen for his friendly assistance, and to David Azrieli for his

ACKNOWLEDGMENTS

generous support. At Scribner, Nan Graham pushed me to rewrite and expand parts of this book, and my thanks to Paul Whitlatch, a fine editor, whose suggestions improved the text, and to Steve Boldt for insightful copyediting. My agent, Andrew Wylie, offered useful advice and formidable support. My wife, Shirley Hallam, was by turns patient and critical, as the need arose.

W.R.
The Icehouse
Chestnut Hill, Philadelphia

Notes

Chapter 1:
Remaking the City

1. The competition finalists included leading landscape firms such as the Olin Partnership, Hargreaves Associates, Ken Smith, and Gustafson Guthrie Nichol.
2. Andrew Blum, "The Active Edge," *Metropolismag.com*, posted February 20, 2006.

Chapter 2:
Three Big Ideas

1. John W. Reps, *The Making of Urban America: A History of City Planning in the United States* (Princeton, N.J.: Princeton University Press, 1965), 111.
2. Jaquelin T. Robertson, "The House as a City," *New Classicism: Omnibus Volume*, ed. Andreas Papadakis and Harriet Wilson (London: Academy Editions, 1990), 234.
3. Quoted by Reps, *Urban America*, 248.
4. Allan Greenberg, *George Washington, Architect* (London: Andreas Papadakis Publisher, 1999), 129.
5. Reps, *Urban America*, 352.
6. Charles Mulford Robinson, "Improvement in City Life: Aesthetic Progress," *Atlantic Monthly* 83 (June 1899): 771.
7. Ibid.
8. Charles Mulford Robinson, "Municipal Art in Paris," *Harper's Magazine* 103 (July 1901): 200–207; "Belgium's Art Crusade,"

Harper's Magazine 104 (February 1902): 443–52; "Art Effort in British Cities," *Harper's Magazine* 105 (October 1902): 787–96.

9. Lewis Mumford, *The City in History: Its Origins, Its Transformations, and Its Prospects* (New York: Harcourt, Brace & World, 1961), 620.

10. Charles Mulford Robinson, *Modern Civic Art: or The City Made Beautiful* (New York: Knickerbocker Press, 1918; orig. pub. 1903), 29.

11. Charles Mulford Robinson, *The Improvement of Towns and Cities: or The Practical Basis of Civic Aesthetics* (New York: Knickerbocker Press, 1901), 286.

12. Robinson, *Modern Civic Art*, 193.

13. Robinson, *Improvement*, 211.

14. Robinson, "Improvement," 772.

15. See William H. Wilson, *The City Beautiful Movement* (Baltimore: Johns Hopkins University Press, 1989).

16. Robert A. M. Stern, *Pride of Place: Building the American Dream* (Boston: Houghton Mifflin, 1986), 307.

17. Robinson, "Improvement," 771.

18. Vincent Scully, *American Architecture and Urbanism* (New York: Henry Holt, 1988; orig. pub. 1969), 138.

19. Witold Rybczynski, "An Open Space of Turf," in *The National Mall: Rethinking Washington's Monumental Core*, ed. Nathan Glazer and Cynthia R. Field (Baltimore: John Hopkins University Press, 2008), 54–65.

20. Robinson, *Modern Civic Art*, 137.

21. "Three Hundred Leading Spring Books," *New York Times*, April 16, 1916.

22. Robinson, *Modern Civic Art*, iii.

23. Greg Hise and William Deerell, *Eden by Design: The 1930 Olmsted-Bartholomew Plan for the Los Angeles Region* (Berkeley: University of California Press, 2000), 292.

24. Witold Rybczynski, *A Clearing in the Distance: Frederick Law Olmsted and America in the Nineteenth Century* (New York: Scribner, 1999), 293.

25. Edward Bellamy, *Looking Backward, 2000-1887*, ed. John L. Thomas (Cambridge, Mass.: Harvard University Press, 1967), 115.

26. Robert Beevers, *The Garden City Utopia: A Critical Biography of Ebenezer Howard* (New York: St. Martin's Press, 1988), 70.

27. Unwin was greatly influenced by the Viennese city planner Camillo Sitte, author of the classic study *The Art of Building Cites: City building according to artistic fundamentals*, trans. Charles T. Stewart (Westport, Conn.: Hyperion Press, 1991; orig. pub. in English 1945; orig. pub. 1889). See also Walter L. Creese, "An Extended Planning Progression," introduction to Raymond Unwin, *Town Planning in Practice: An Introduction to the Art of Designing Cities and Suburbs* (New York: Princeton Architectural Press, 1994; orig. pub. 1909), xii–xiii.

28. Robert A. M. Stern and John Montague Massengale, eds., *The Anglo-American Suburb* (London: Architectural Design Profile, 1981), 42.

29. Robert W. de Forest to Frederick Law Olmsted Jr., December 7, 1908, Rockefeller Archive, Pocantico Hills, N.Y.

30. Frederick Law Olmsted Jr. to Robert W. de Forest, December 20, 1908, Rockefeller Archive, Pocantico Hills, N.Y.

31. For a history of Forest Hills see Susan L. Klaus, *A Modern Arcadia: Frederick Law Olmsted, Jr. & the Plan for Forest Hills Gardens* (Amherst and Boston: University of Massachusetts Press, 2002), 31.

32. See Peter Pennoyer and Anne Walker, *The Architecture of Grosvenor Atterbury* (New York: W. W. Norton & Company, 2009), 81–82.

33. Ibid., 176.

34. De Forest to Olmsted, December 20, 1908.

35. Pennoyer and Walker, *Grosvenor Atterbury*, 158.

36. Lewis Mumford, "Mass-Production and the Modern House," *Architectural Record*, January 1930, 110-16.

37. De Forest to Olmsted, December 20, 1908.

38. Stern, *Pride of Place*, 143.

39. These projects are described in Stern and Massengale, *Anglo-American Suburb*.

40. Le Corbusier and Pierre Jeanneret, *Oeuvre Complète de 1910-1929* (Zurich: Les Éditions d'Architecture Erlenbach, 1946), 34.

41. Le Corbusier, *The City of Tomorrow and Its Planning*, trans. Frederick Etchells (New York: Dover, 1987; orig. pub. in English 1929; orig. pub. 1925), 163.

42. Le Corbusier and Jeanneret, *Oeuvre Complète*, 34.

43. Ibid., 104.

44. See Le Corbusier, *City*, 278–79; Kenneth Frampton, *Le Cor-*

busier: Architect of the Twentieth Century (New York: Harry N. Abrams, 2002), 3.33.

45. Le Corbusier, *City*, 281.
46. Ibid., 177.
47. W. Franklyn Paris, "The International Exposition of Modern Industrial and Decorative Art," *Architectural Record* 58, no. 4 (October 1925): 365–85.
48. *Encyclopédie des Arts Décoratifs et Industriels Modernes au XXème Siècle, vol. 2: Architecture* (Paris: Imprimerie Nationale, 1925), 44–45.
49. Le Corbusier, *City*, 8.
50. Le Corbusier, *La Ville Radieuse* (Paris: Vincent, Fréal & Cie., 1964; orig. pub. 1933), 104. Translated by author.
51. Charles Jencks, *Le Corbusier and the Tragic View of Architecture* (Cambridge, Mass.: Harvard University Press, 1973), 120.
52. Robert Hughes, *The Shock of the New* (New York: Alfred A. Knopf, 1991), 191.
53. A description of the Futurama is included in David Gelernter, *1939: The Lost World of the Fair* (New York: The Free Press, 1995), 19-25.
54. Alexander Garvin, *The American City: What Works, What Doesn't* (New York: McGraw-Hill, 1996), 124.

Chapter 3:
Home Remedies

1. For example, Jane Jacobs, "Washington," *Architectural Forum*, January 1956, 93–115; "Typical Downtown Transformed," *Architectural Forum*, May 1956, 145–55.
2. Jane Jacobs, "The Missing Link in City Redevelopment," *Architectural Forum*, June 1956, 133.
3. Lewis Mumford, "Home Remedies for Urban Cancer," in *The Lewis Mumford Reader*, ed. Donald L. Miller (New York: Pantheon Books, 1986), 186. Orig. pub. as "Mother Jacobs' Home Remedies," *New Yorker*, December 1, 1962.
4. Alice Sparberg Alexiou, *Jane Jacobs: Urban Visionary* (New Brunswick, N.J.: Rutgers University Press, 2006), 61–62.
5. William H. Whyte Jr. "Are Cities Un-American?" *Fortune*, September 1957, 124.

6. Alexiou, *Jacobs*, 62-63.
7. Jane Jacobs, "Downtown Is for People," *Fortune*, April 1958, 133.
8. Ibid., 242.
9. Harrison E. Salisbury, review of *The Exploding Metropolis*, *New York Times Book Review*, October 5, 1958.
10. Nathan Glazer, "Why City Planning Is Obsolete," *Architectural Forum*, July 1958, 96.
11. Ibid., 97.
12. Ibid., 98.
13. Epstein had recently joined Random House after founding Anchor Books, where he had published *The Exploding Metropolis*.
14. Jane Jacobs, *The Death and Life of Great American Cities* (New York: Random House, 1961), 3.
15. Ibid., 25.
16. Ibid., 19.
17. Ibid., 23.
18. Ibid., 87–88.
19. Ibid., 372.
20. Lloyd Rodwin, review of *The Death and Life of Great American Cities*, *New York Times Book Review*, November 5, 1961.
21. Jacobs, *Death and Life*, 20.
22. Mumford, "Home Remedies," 196.
23. Ibid., 194.
24. Ibid., 197.
25. Ibid., 191.
26. Ibid., 197.
27. Jacobs, *Death and Life*, 376–77.
28. Ibid., 391.

Chapter 4:
Mr. Wright and the Disappearing City

1. Frank Lloyd Wright, *Modern Architecture, Being the Kahn Lectures for 1930* (Princeton: Princeton University Press, 1931), 101.
2. Ibid., 110.
3. Ibid., 103.
4. Le Corbusier, "A Noted Architect Dissects Our Cities," *New York Times Magazine*, January 3, 1932, 10.

5. Ibid.

6. Meryle Secrest, *Frank Lloyd Wright* (New York: Alfred A. Knopf, 1992), 392–94.

7. Frank Lloyd Wright, "Towards a New Architecture," *World Unity*, September 1928, in *Frank Lloyd Wright Collected Writings, Vol. 1, 1894–1930*, ed. Bruce Brooks Pfeiffer (New York: Rizzoli, 1992), 317–18.

8. Frank Lloyd Wright, "Broadacre City: An Architect's Vision," *New York Times Magazine*, March 20, 1932, 8.

9. Portions of Wright's *New York Times* essay, which contained specific rebuttals to Le Corbusier's previous article, appear verbatim in *The Disappearing City*.

10. Frank Lloyd Wright, *The Disappearing City* (New York: William Farquhar Payson, 1932), 17.

11. Ibid., 31.

12. Catherine K. Bauer, "When Is a House Not a House?" *Nation* 136 (January 25, 1933): 99–100.

13. R. L. Duffus, review of *The Disappearing City*, *New York Times Book Review*, December 11, 1932, 3.

14. Frank Lloyd Wright, *The Living City* (New York: New American Library, 1970; orig. pub. 1958), 230.

15. George Fred Keck, review of *The Disappearing City*, *Journal of Land & Public Utility Economics* 9, no. 2 (May 1933): 16.

16. Lewis Mumford, "The Ideal Form of the Modern City" in *The Lewis Mumford Reader*, ed. Donald L. Miller (New York: Pantheon Books, 1986), 163. Orig. pub. as "The Modern City," in *Forms and Functions of Twentieth-Century Architecture*, vol. 4, *Building Types*, ed. Talbot Hamlin (New York: Columbia University Press, 1952).

17. David G. De Long, "Frank Lloyd Wright and the Evolution of the Living City," in *Frank Lloyd Wright and the Living City*, ed. David G. De Long (Milan: Skira Editore, 1998), 42.

18. Frank Lloyd Wright, *When Democracy Builds* (Chicago: University of Chicago Press, 1945), 121.

19. Quoted in Brendan Gill, *Many Masks: A Life of Frank Lloyd Wright* (New York: G. P. Putnam's Sons, 1987), 477.

Chapter 5:
The Demand-Side of Urbanism

1. Michael Barone, "The Seventies Shift," *The Wilson Quarterly* 33, no. 4 (Autumn 2009): 42.

2. Jon C. Teaford, *The Twentieth-Century American City: Problem, Promise, and Reality* (Baltimore: Johns Hopkins University Press, 1986), 127-50.

3. Alexander Garvin, *The American City: What Works, What Doesn't* (New York: McGraw-Hill, 1996), 1.

4. Ibid., 2.

5. Lewis Mumford, "Yesterday's City of Tomorrow," in *The Lewis Mumford Reader*, ed. Donald L. Miller (New York: Pantheon Books, 1986), 181. Orig. pub. as "The Future of the City: Part 2—Yesterday's City of Tomorrow," *Architectural Record* 132, no. 5 (November 1962).

6. Discussed more fully in Witold Rybczynski, "Bauhaus Blunders," *Public Interest* 113 (Fall 1993): 82–90.

7. Jonathan Barnett, *The Elusive City: Five Centuries of Design, Ambition and Miscalculation* (New York: Harper & Row, 1986), 238.

8. Jane Jacobs, *The Death and Life of Great American Cities* (New York: Random House, 1961), 269.

9. Witold Rybczynski, "America's Favorite Buildings," *Wharton Real Estate Review* 11, no. 2 (Fall 2007): 94–105.

10. For example, Chestnut Hill in Philadelphia, Shaker Heights in Cleveland, Country Club District in Kansas City, Beverly Hills and Palos Verdes in Los Angeles, River Oaks in Houston, Druid Hills in Atlanta, and Coral Gables in Miami.

11. Elizabeth Hawes, *New York, New York: How the Apartment House Transformed the Life of the City (1869–1930)* (New York: Alfred A. Knopf, 1993), ch. 4.

12. Apartment living took hold in New York in 1927. "That year, for the first time in a century, the Building Department did not receive a single application for permission to build a private house for six months." Ibid., 237.

13. Jacobs, *Death and Life*, 448.

14. Roger Montgomery, "Is There Still Life in the Death and Life?" *Journal of the American Planning Association* 64, no. 3 (Summer 1998): 275.

15. See Herbert J. Gans, "Jane Jacobs: Toward an Understanding of 'Death and Life of Great American Cities,'" *City & Community* 5, no. 3 (September 2006): 213.
16. Herbert J. Gans, "City Planning and Urban Realities," *Commentary* 33 (1962): 173.
17. Ibid., 172.
18. Ibid.
19. Jacobs, *Death and Life*, 391.
20. Vincent Scully, "The Architecture of Community," in *The New Urbanism: Toward an Architecture of Community*, ed. Peter Katz (New York: McGraw-Hill, 1994), 221.
21. Martin Meyerson et al., *The Face of the Metropolis* (New York: Random House, 1968), 23.
22. Andrejs Skaburskis, "New Urbanism and Sprawl: A Toronto Case Study," *Journal of Planning Education and Research* 25 (2006): 233.

Chapter 6:
Arcades and Malls, Big Boxes
and Lifestyle Centers

1. Nicolas Brazier, *Histoire des petits théâtres de Paris* (Paris: Allardin, 1838),105.
2. Victor Gruen, *The Heart of Our Cities: The Urban Crisis: Diagnosis and Cure* (New York: Simon & Schuster, 1964), 194.
3. Joel Garreau, *Edge City: Life on the New Frontier* (New York: Doubleday, 1991), 465.
4. Jonathan Barnett, *Redesigning Cities: Principles, Practice, Implementation* (Chicago: Planners Press, 2003), 52.
5. For example, ZCMI Center in Salt Lake City, Water Tower Place in Chicago, the Gallery at Market East in Philadelphia, Stamford Town Center in Stamford, Connecticut, and Horton Plaza in San Diego.
6. Bernard J. Frieden and Lynne B. Sagalyn, *Downtown, Inc.: How America Rebuilds Cities* (Cambridge, Mass.: MIT Press, 1992), 311-12 .
7. Peter Linneman and Deborah C. Moy, "The Evolution of Retailing in the United States," *Wharton Real Estate Review* 7, no. 1 (Spring 2003): 50.

8. Phil Patton, *Made in USA: The Secret Histories of the Things That Made America* (New York: Grove Weidenfeld, 1992), 252–64.
9. Although the term *lifestyle center* is said to have been coined by a Memphis-based developer, Poag & McEwen, in the late 1980s, lifestyle centers did not become popular until the following decade.
10. David Dillon, "Dallas experiments with instant urbanism at Victory," *Architectural Record*, October 2006, 82.
11. See also Victoria Gardens in Rancho Cucamonga, California, and Crocker Park in Westlake, Ohio.
12. Elsa Brenner, "A Piazza for a Maryland Suburb," *New York Times*, November 22, 2006, C7.
13. Lake Anne Village, with housing clusters designed by Washington, D.C., architect Charles M. Goodman, was the only village to adopt a modernist layout. Other village centers at Reston resemble conventional strip malls.
14. Alan Ward, "Certainty to Flexibility: Planning and Design History, 1963-2005," in *Reston Town Center: A Downtown for the 21st Century*, ed. Alan Ward (Washington, D.C.: Academy Press, 2006), 40.
15. Ibid., 73.
16. Garreau, *Edge City*.
17. Ibid., 3.
18. Robert A. M. Stern, "Designing the Suburban City," in *Reston Town Center*, 173.

Chapter 7:
On the Waterfront

1. Le Corbusier, *The City of Tomorrow and Its Planning*, trans. Frederick Etchells (New York: Dover, 1987; orig. pub. in English 1929; orig. pub. in French 1925), 165.
2. William H. Wilson, *The City Beautiful Movement* (Baltimore: Johns Hopkins University Press, 1989), 128.
3. Robin Karson, *A Genius for Place: American Landscape for the Country Place Era*, Library of American Landscape History (Amherst: University of Massachusetts Press, 2007), 25.
4. Wilson, *City Beautiful*, 146.
5. Karson, *Genius*, 36.

NOTES

6. Wilson, *City Beautiful*, 139.
7. Daniel H. Burnham and Edward H. Bennett, *Plan of Chicago* (New York: Princeton Architectural Press, 1993; orig. pub. 1909), 97.
8. Marc Levinson, *The Box: How the Shipping Container Made the World Smaller and the World Economy Bigger* (Princeton, N.J.: Princeton University Press, 2006), 48–53.
9. Ibid., 96.
10. Alexander Garvin, *The American City: What Works, What Doesn't* (New York: McGraw-Hill, 1996), 112.
11. Ibid., 53–54.

Chapter 8:
The Bilbao Anomaly

1. Ann L. Strong and George E. Thomas, *The Book of the School: 100 Years of the Graduate School of Fine Arts of the University of Pennsylvania* (Philadelphia: GSFA, 1990), 141.
2. The case for a piecemeal approach to urban design is argued by Christopher Alexander et al., *A New Theory of Urban Design* (New York: Oxford University Press, 1987).
3. "The Downtown We Don't Want," *New York Times*, July 17, 2002, A18.
4. Paul Goldberger, "The Sky Line: Groundwork," *New Yorker*, May 20, 2002, 91.
5. Edward Wyatt, "Officials Rethink Building Proposal for Ground Zero," *New York Times*, July 21, 2002, A1.
6. Quoted by Paul Goldberger, "The Sky Line: Designing Downtown," *New Yorker*, January 6, 2003, 90.
7. Jane Jacobs, *The Death and Life of Great American Cities* (New York: Random House, 1961), 25.
8. Philip Nobel, *Sixteen Acres: Architecture and the Outrageous Struggle for the Future of Ground Zero* (New York: Metropolitan Books, 2005), 115.
9. Barry Bergdoll, *European Architecture, 1750-1890* (Oxford: Oxford University Press, 2000), 269-79.
10. Ibid., 276.
11. Charles Jencks, *The Iconic Building* (New York: Rizzoli, 2005), 33.

12. Ibid., 12.
13. Quoted by Sheri Olson, "For the Bellevue Arts Museum, which values making art as well as viewing it, Steven Holl invented a place that engages visitors with architecture—and with one another," *Architectural Record*, August 2001, 81.
14. Nobel, *Sixteen Acres*, 26.
15. Witold Rybczynski, "America's Favorite Buildings," *Wharton Real Estate Review* 11, no. 2 (Fall 2007): 97.
16. Dorothy Spears, "When the Final Touch Is the Exit Door," *New York Times*, March 12, 2008, H1.
17. Ibid.
18. Olson, "Bellevue Arts Museum," 81.
19. Spears, "Final Touch," H1. The Bellevue Arts Museum reopened in 2005 as a museum of craft and design.
20. Inga Saffron, "In the Kimmel, an idea that exceeded reality," *Philadelphia Inquirer*, December 4, 2005, C1. The suit was settled out of court.
21. Nobel, *Sixteen Acres*, 184.
22. Ada Louise Huxtable, "Rebuilding Lower Manhattan," in *On Architecture: Collected Reflections on a Century of Change* (New York: Walker & Company, 2008), 387.
23. David W. Dunlap, "At Rail Hub, Bird Will Still Soar, but with a Bit Less Polish," *New York Times*, May 8, 2008, B2.

Chapter 9:
Putting the Pieces Together

1. Robert Bruegmann, *Sprawl: A Compact History* (Chicago: University of Chicago Press, 2005), 26–27.
2. Nicholas Confessore, "Cities Grow Up, and Some See Sprawl," *New York Times*, August 6, 2006.
3. Jonathan Barnett, *Redesigning Cities: Principles, Practice, Implementation* (Chicago: Planners Press, 2003), 36–39.
4. Lisa Chamberlain, "Building a City Within the City of Atlanta," *New York Times*, May 24, 2006.
5. Quoted in Brent W. Ambrose and William Grigsby, "Mixed Income Groups in Public Housing," *Wharton Real Estate Review* 3, no. 2 (Fall 1999): 7.

Chapter 10:
The Kind of Cities We Want

1. Mayor Rendell's talk took place on April 9, 1996, at the Rittenhouse Hotel.
2. John W. Reps, *The Making of Urban America: A History of City Planning in the United States* (Princeton, N.J.: Princeton University Press, 1965), 90.
3. Andres Duany, Elizabeth Plater-Zyberk, and Jeff Speck, *Suburban Nation: The Rise of Sprawl and the Decline of the American Dream* (New York: North Point Press, 2000).
4. *Denver Tops List of Favorite Cities*, A Social and Demographic Trends Report (Washington, D.C.: Pew Research Center, January 29, 2009), 3.
5. According to the U.S. Census, between 1980 and 2006, the population grew from 227 million to 300 million (an increase of 32 percent), while the number of people living in cities larger than one hundred thousand grew from 51 million to 81 million (an increase of 59 percent).
6. Irving Kristol, "Urban Civilization & Its Discontents," *Commentary* 50 (July 1970): 31.
7. Ibid.
8. Office of Technology Assessment, *The Technological Reshaping of Metropolitan America* (Washington, D.C.: U.S. Government Printing Office, September 1995), 12.
9. Edward L. Glaeser, "Houston, New York Has a Problem," *New York Sun*, July 16, 2008, 4.
10. Ibid.
11. *Denver Tops List*, 5.
12. David Brooks, "I Dream of Denver," *New York Times*, February 17, 2009, A29.
13. See Blake Gumprecht, *The American College Town* (Amherst, Mass.: University of Massachusetts Press, 2008).
14. Kristol, "Urban Civilization," 31.
15. According to the U.S. Census, the total number of people living in cities larger than 250,000 was 39.4 million in 1960, 42.3 million in 1970, and 52.1 million in 2006. The corresponding figures for cities between 25,000 and 250,000 were 36.6 million in 1960, 45.8 million in 1970, and 81.7 million in 2006. Measured

as a percentage of the total population living in cities (115.9 million in 1960, and 186.1 million in 2006), the big cities' share dropped from 34.0 percent in 1960 to 28.0 percent in 2006, whereas the small cities' share rose from 31.6 percent in 1960 to 43.9 percent in 2006.

16. *Denver Tops List*, 5.
17. Joel Garreau, "Face-to-Face Places," *Wharton Real Estate Review* 12, no. 1 (Spring 2008): 73.
18. Ibid.
19. "The 2008 Global Cities Index," *Foreign Policy*, November/December 2008.
20. Edward L. Glaeser, "Why Economists Still Like Cities," *City Journal*, Spring 1996, 44.
21. Eugenie Ladner Birch, "Having a Longer View on Downtown Living," Journal of the American Planning Association 68, no. 1 (2002): 5–21.
22. Eugenie Ladner Birch, "Who Lives Downtown?" Living Cities Census Series (Washington, D.C.: The Brookings Institution, November 2005), 5.
23. Ibid., 7.
24. Joel Kotkin, *The City: A Global History* (New York: Modern Library, 2005), xvii.

Chapter 11:
The Kind of Cities We Need

1. Clifford Krauss, "Gas Prices Send Surge of Riders to Mass Transit," *New York Times*, May 10, 2008, A1.
2. Alan Pisarski, *Commuting in America III*, Transportation Research Board study, October 16, 2006. http://onlinepubs.trb.org/onlinepubs/nchrp/CIAIIIfacts.pdf.
3. Bill Vlasic and Nick Bunkley, "Toyota Scales Back Production of Big Vehicles," *New York Times*, July 11, 2008, C1.
4. Department of Transportation press release, August 26, 2009, http://www.dot.gov/affairs/2009/dot13309.htm.
5. David Owen, *Green Metropolis: Why Living Smaller, Living Closer, and Driving Less Are the Keys to Sustainability* (New York: Riverhead Books, 2009), 2–3.
6. Ibid., 285.

7. Timothy Beatley, *Green Urbanism: Learning from European Cities* (Washington, D.C.: Island Press, 2000), 4–5.
8. Ibid., 3–4.
9. Moshe Safdie, *For Everyone a Garden* (Cambridge, Mass.: MIT Press, 1974), 4.
10. Lewis Mumford, "The Disappearing City," in *The Lewis Mumford Reader*, ed. Donald L. Miller (New York: Pantheon Books, 1986), 112. Orig. pub. as "The Future of the City: Part I—the Disappearing City," *Architectural Record* 132, no. 4 (October 1962).
11. Lewis Mumford, "The Choices Ahead," in Miller, *Lewis Mumford Reader*, 239. Orig. pub. in *The Urban Prospect: Essays* (New York: Harcourt Brace and World, 1968).

List of Illustrations

Photographic acknowledgments are given in parentheses. Every effort has been made to contact all copyright holders. The publishers will be happy to make good in future editions any errors or omissions brought to their attention.

Index

INDEX